Above the Colonial Subconscious, Africa Moves

Michel Ngue-Awane

Clink
Street

London | New York

Published by Clink Street Publishing 2015

Copyright © 2015

First edition.

ISBN: 978-1-910782-65-1
E-book: 978-1-910782-66-8

Table of Contents

Part Two: Our Plan Together Here and Now

Part Three: A New Dawn

Extract

Above the Colonial Subconscious, Africa Moves

The journey began with the fight for independence and ended with freedom and progress when we understood that the battlefield was in the mind. Though we won the physical battle against the colonial powers' occupation, we struggled to liberate our minds as a result of derogating, subtle and systematic programming of our subconscious through systems, methods and programmes put in place to control us. The colonial subconscious takes us through a journey of self-discovery. A journey where most pitfalls are unconsciously dug by ourselves and its discoveries lead us to a stage of self-actualisation where we finally reach a period of consciousness, taking a firm decision to be ourselves and act together for our common good. Finally aware of self, the prevailing situation, our potential and power within, we are determined to take full charge of our destinies, rising above all prejudices and stereotypes, advocating for reparation damages whilst rejecting all forms of subjugations and sub-human treatments, we change our strategies to win; holding tight to our memorandum of hope, our guiding principle to the top. Africa moves above the colonial subconscious, standing tall where everyone else comes short. We lead the way as we did since mankind was created. After all, the first man was born here and the first great civilisation started here; for now, we have all we need to be who we are and want to become. The journey has started and the destination is known. We are moving above the colonial subconscious!

MICHEL NGUE-AWANE

Acknowledgements

To my wife, **Annie** you have been my inspiration and motivation for continuing to improve my knowledge and my career advancement. I thank you for all your support.

To my children, **Michele Kem**, **Tanya** and **Ashley Sandra** you bring so much joy to my life and you are the reason why I strive for excellence and achievement. I hope I will inspire you to aim high in life.

Special thanks to you, **Kemia (Michele Kem)** after reading the first chapter you suggested I change one of the character's name. You were right.

To **Dr Apollinaire Lekeuneu**, friend, Brother and mentor; your encouragements and belief in me have made me who I am, striving to be the best, and my love for you is unquestionable.

To **Mrs Esther Dollinger**, my sister, I appreciate your constant support and belief in me.

To **Sian, Mafiamba** whilst this book was underway, you linked me up with so many people and I appreciate you selflessness.

To my fellow writer **Andre Ekama**, from Germany. I appreciate your input in terms of advice.

I thank God Almighty for his inspiration. Without the help of the Holy Spirit, I wouldn't have completed this book and Jesus Christ remains my Lord, my rock and salvation. Most of the principles of this book are based on the Bible teachings. To he who believes, nothing is impossible.

Selected Notes/Comments

I am proud of you, my dear friend Michel Ngue-Awane and I agreed with what you say in this book. Your analysis is pertinent and I entirely adhere to your vision of offloading ourselves from tars that obstruct our vision for a better Africa. This book contributes to the awakening of our young Africans' conscience and will help in building a new Africa of peace, integrated freedom, unity and prosperity.

All the best and I have hope that this book will touch the heart of many as it reshapes and contributes to the whole debate of a better Africa in the media and where discussion takes place on the future of Africa.

Fulgence Abdou Tanga Kabore,

(General Secretary of the Federation of Clubs and African Union Associations)

Dear Michel

I would like to extend my sincere thanks and congratulate you for accepting our invitation at Afrique Media TV. After your intervention in our platform, our listeners' and viewers' reactions are overwhelming. Particularly the reaction of our viewers who watched you live. They all support your endeavour and command you resolve to engage in a rebirth of the pan-Africanism through the use of your pen. Once again I congratulate you.

Ladan Mahommed Bachir, Journalist, Afrique Media.

This book is an honourable initiative and the key facts discussed in this book show that despite the time elapsed, our history follows us and our children. If people understand the aims of this book, the battle will be won. However, compensation alone will not heal our wounds. Despite the hurts and torts of the colonial era, there were some positive outcomes. We need to have some sort of introspection to understand that we are to blame for some of our demises. Let's shift our focus on how to build our infrastructures in order to overcome unemployment that prevents us from developing. It is best for now to move forward, though our past will never go away.

Josiane Mouigni – Executive assistant, Africa news Network Multimédia Sarl / KALAK FM

Preface of the book: Above the colonial subconscious, Africa Moves.

When I first glanced inside this book, I laughed; when I read more pages, I smiled and when I read deeper I faded off and my reading ended with cries and remorse. Not only because of the quality and level of the reflection caused by its content, but also because of the truth, the veracity of it. Immediately, what came into my mind is this statement from the apostle Paul: I die daily. This is one of the most philosophical statements ever to exist in my opinion and that should be our motive and our driven purpose for life.

From my own perspective, what Paul means by that is our perpetual questioning of our purpose in this life, on a daily basis. To understand today' death, we have to revisit yesterday, a renaissance. But, revealing your real feeling is the starting point of your healing process. Using the subconscious mind-set to establish your continuum can perhaps be an open door to your real existence. The reality is the conversation one can have with oneself about one's real nature and driven purpose for life. Who are you and where are you going? Those are the questions.

Is the author a sort of countryside lawyer, villagers' lawyer or simple a street lawyer? The reason I mentioned this is because whoever is addressed in this book is part of it and, as stakeholders, they are all accountable for the success of their community wherever they are: our conscience on the unconsciousness of our existence. This book has so many themes and so many openings that will open doors to real life.

Who really reads the preface of a book? Not many people, but for this particular one, I hope students in general, students enrolled in international relations and/or African studies, researchers in political science, philosophical studies and economy, investors, teachers, invaders, oppressors, oppressed and so on will do so. If that is you, I guarantee that the preface is way less interesting than the book itself and if you are eager to consume pages of it before it gets dark, run and continue to read the book to find out your purpose and come back here later because it is what it is all about.

Let's first talk about the author: I have known Michel Ngue-Awane since he was two hours old; from this early on because I was at the neighbour's house when he came into the world, and since then, I have watched him grow as a baby, a toddler, a young boy, teenager and, then, as the man. There has always been something special about him that I admired and I bet most people who know him will agree with me: determination.

Dr Appolinaire Lekeuneu, Buffalo, New York, USA

Part One:

Our Journey Begins

Chapter 1:

The call was answered and ended with despair

I was tired and upset. So, too, were my six brothers. At this time we were uncertain little children whose only demand was the right to run around in the open. The wait was too long for us to bear, having stood at the same place waiting for a car that was nowhere to be seen for over five hours, and with nothing to do; we became restless in that parents forbade even just crossing the road or running around.

Looking up, I could see a wonderful scene, which demanded an unwavering gaze; a fiery red orb of light slowly sinking beneath the horizon; threads of light lingering in the sky, mingling with the rolling clouds, dyeing the heavens first orange, then red, then dark blue, until all that was left of the sun was a chalky mauve.

The sun had started to find its way back home, easing behind the mountain whilst blinking its eyes. Tired and giving up his hope of riding on four wheels down to his village, my dad, Mbii, after a vain five-hour wait for a car, decided to take the road to Mengan on foot.

It took some time for him to decide as there was still hope that at least one car would eventually take our direction. Despite the wait, nothing changed and Dad finally made up his mind. But before we could leave town, the sun had begun closing its eyes, melting away in intermittence as stygian darkness took over the sky. Sequin-silver stars like the glowing embers of a dying fire soon winked down at me, illuminating the atramentous curtain of sky, then suddenly the clouds parted, and I found myself looking at a lustrous, argent disc casting brilliant rays of moonlight onto the dark grounds. What wonderful magic from Mother Nature! At this time of the year, the sun usually goes to sleep between 6.30 and 7 pm. This means, anyhow, we were somewhere close to 7 pm; however, undeterred by the darkness that had suddenly taken the place, my dad took us through a small path leading to a tiny village in the middle of the forest in the south west of the country. We were heading to Mengan, from where our last ancestors could be traced and which, I was now told, would be my new home.

I wasn't born there but I was told that I was from there, and this knowledge gives me a reference point in life. I was also told later that some of my forefathers, brothers and sisters will never trace their roots or know exactly from which part of our continent they came because they were forcefully dragged out of our lands to far away west, where they helped build the greatest nation on earth, and where till now they have never been recognised or praised for their endeavours. Until now, despite our cries for justice and our cries for recognition, no one has ever apologised or paid for damages caused to our land. A land used and dumped, sucked at will of all goods that it holds as presents from God, the creator.

Our journey was a defining moment in our lives, yet we as kids were completely unaware of upcoming changes. To us it was a moment like any other, though a deciding moment in our lives. This was the day where Dad and Mum, I and my six brothers were returning to the village

Dad left over 20 years before to help his country fight for independence and restore peace. He left as a teenager and was returning as a man. Since leaving the village, he had regularly returned home, but had not gone back in the last five years due to his army duty, which did not leave him much time to return as often as before. Perhaps, if Grandma had still been around, Dad would have found time to visit, but her passing away created a void in Dad's heart and he saw no reason for regular trips to the village.

On this day of his first visit in five years after Grandma's crossing to eternity, and our first in our entire life, sadness was written all over my mum's and dad's faces. Dad was saddened by losing his job without notice and without any rewards, saddened about the separation from his friends he had worked with for over ten years, aggrieved by lack and the poverty that was already taking his toll on him, just weeks after losing his job, and concerned about his future and ours; he was heading remorsefully to his native forest village.

Mum, on the other hand, was saddened because she dreaded returning to the unproductive farm work. Amongst her friends, she had been considered as fortunate when she married someone who lived in a city. But now that she was returning to her native land, she would have no choice but to re-join her ancestors' profession – subsistence farming – which requires a lot of hard work and yields little return. Subsistence farmers never had enough to meet their own needs and they lived perpetually in poverty. They aged very early, and most of them died before they reached their sixties. Mum had, at least for the time she was in the city, forgotten about this hard life. In the city, she didn't have to wake up early in the morning and go to the farm and return at night, tired, to have a little sleep and wake up the next morning to start the same process. In the city, she could buy produce from the village and she didn't have to do the hard work. She couldn't imagine how her life would become in the village and she hoped that, by some mysterious powers, the situation would turn around. This was a vain hope and she had to accept what waited ahead.

Dad couldn't believe what was happening to him. Twenty years ago, the whole country was in turmoil and all native citizens were called to show a sense of patriotism and fight against the enemies of independence; those who everyone believed were against peace and stability in the land. Aged only 18, he accepted the call of duty and enrolled in the army as a commando where, after a brief induction, he was sent to battle fronts in various areas of the country. Soldiers, as well as all people of the country, were promised a better life after the independence. They were told that the independences would bring freedom, prosperity and a better future for all. It was repeatedly proclaimed that poverty would become history and that resources endowed by Mother Nature to this great country would serve its inhabitants once the invaders were gone.

It was clear in my father's mind as he recalled that, if this was going to be the case for everyone, soldiers would be better off. They were told that the country was rich with natural resources – which is true – and that the only reason common citizens did not enjoy it was down to the colonial powers which exploited everything for themselves; but once they were gone, they said, the land would be managed by us and our resources would be used for the benefit of all citizens. This thought alone made everyone dream of a new paradise. Some even interpreted that as meaning that in the new state they wouldn't have to work at all, but would get what they wanted at will.

Now, having served for 20 years and having helped

bring peace, he was returning to the village empty handed. He had no provisions for the next day and no hope for tomorrow. When he was a soldier, he was housed in the army barracks and fed; he had a small salary and got married. In his 14 years of marriage, he had seven children and was taking them back to his native village, knowing not where the next morning's dinner would come from. I mean, next day – how about next week or next year? He knew not and his wife dared not to ask, even though this question was bothering her mind.

On the way I and my brothers had many questions; many were asked, at times with answers, but most of the time, no answers were given. However, Dad had no choice but to give us some hope in order to feed our curiosity as we looked forward to settling in this much-talked-about village.

Children are always excited when they hear about new things but when they are travelling, they are even more excited. Like any other children, we were looking forward to this day but our euphoria on reaching Newtown, the closest city to the village, did not last long. The gentle sunset on that afternoon may have given it an appearance of normal life but as we waited for the village's cars, we found the apparent normal life to be a shell. We witnessed at least four different fights amongst citizens and observed brutality from the so-called anti-gang forces. To us they were soldiers, but what was striking was that their behaviour was not honourable at all, even to my child's eyes. As he murmured and sighed, dad informed us that most of these people were those who had organised themselves to defend this city during troubled times, and who had become high street robbers. During the independence, they defended the city very well hoping that, with the departure of the colonisers, they would have jobs as was promised, but no one remembered them and they took hold of the city. The city became prone to spasms of brutal anarchy and chaotically administered public services by these new bosses who took over without any formal training, vision, or planning. They thought that the treasury was full of inexhaustible supplies of money. What they found in place was quickly embezzled and they soon found themselves out of supplies, having gotten used to the high life. It was only for them to they identify new sources of revenues. Unfortunately, only normal citizens paid the price for their folly.

Anyone in a position of responsibility defended their right to eat and use what could be obtained, legally or not, to feed the needs of the present in the wait for tomorrow, where they started the same and so on. They inherited a system about which they knew nothing, and maintaining this system was becoming too much for them.

To his bigger surprise, Dad could not find any car to our village. If he had only known that things had changed so badly, he wouldn't have come back with the entire family – which had increased tremendously in the last five years with the addition of three more children.

Walking in the jungle-like territory, we were sweating, falling and rising up, not giving up at this time, where the raining season had ended and, following a dry day, dusk had started to answer the call of winds. By now, the wind – carrying all sorts of debris – forced us to sneeze often. We had just left the main city and were continuing to the village by foot after five hours' wait in vain for a car that used to go to his village. Up to five years ago, he could take the car to this village, but Dad was surprised how quickly things had changed. Frustrated after 5 hours wait, Dad tried to enquire why there was no car heading to his village and he was told that bridges have ceded and no car was able to cross the many rivers that lead to his village, leaving people no choice but to walk or cycle to Mengan and beyond.

With seven children and all that he brought from the army, he had no choice but to proceed at a convenient rhythm for the family. He remembered that just 20 years ago, when the Europeans were still in the country, there was a big road leading to far away villages through his village. People were often forced to dig the roads by hand and those roads were regularly maintained. Every weekend, there was human investment, whereby all villagers came together and give their time free for community work. This helped the entire village progress. Beside villagers' wilful contribution, they were often forced to work in big programmes and projects instigated by the central administration, under the colonial power. Roads were built through forced labour. The colonial powers used it to access the villages they ruled, but everyday users were the locals.

If my parents knew that there wouldn't be cars to their village, they would have prepared themselves, they said. For example, they would have done the trip in two or three separate journeys at day time to spare us such misery of trotting in the middle of the forest at night. But now that we were already on our way, we had no choice to continue, as we progressed and did our best to get to the village. We were advancing in the deep of the forest, where trees as tall as three storey buildings often blocked our way, and because the forest here was very fecund, it was difficult to move faster. The path we were walking on was the remainder of the main road between Newton and Mela, a faraway town in the west, and Mengan was a village in between where Mbii, my dad, was born. "This road used to be the main road leading to Mela with regular four-wheeled traffic, when the western colonisers were still in charge and up to five years ago," he said. Even five years ago, despite the degradation of the road, it was still accessible by car; but it is astonishing how much worse the road had become. For the most part of the journey, we progressed in silence, even when familiar landmarks from the past flashed back; Dad said no words, as it was now a new experience for him. None of us had ever been to this village and our excitement was turning into disappointment as, tired of walking, we started crying.

Our village was just seven miles from the main town, but at this rhythm, it could take the whole night to get there. Luckily, along the road, there were several villages and people who could host us for a night so we could continue our journey the next morning. We tried to go as far as we could but around 9 pm we stopped somewhere for the night as we became tired, hungry, and unwilling to move a foot further.

Ten years ago, when Dad visited the village, the road had started degrading and there was a lot of talk about how the work to rebuild it would start soon. Five years ago, when he returned, it was exactly during the general electoral campaign and the rebuilding of the road was one of several promises made to the villagers. The villages along this road were even visited, one by one, by the new governor, who travelled all the way to Mela promising that the construction would start soon. When he visited, he reassured the villagers that the president had sent him to inform them that he was aware of the state of the roads, and that not only the road, but new schools would be built. Each time the governor visited, he went home with the villagers' precious possessions – cattle, goats, chicken, pork, food – and he was even attributed plot of lands in each village. Children were named after him and some people prided themselves to have had a head-to-head talk with the governor. They were his friends and he knew them by name. But in five years, two different governors came and went, and no one had heard about when the big project would start.

Dad was probably prepared for anything but he was not at all prepared to find out that the road to his village had disappeared so suddenly. It is surprising how any goods badly maintained can be lost forever. As we progressed, he asked himself, how do other villagers beyond Mengan ever get to their remote villages, how do people now get to Mela? He couldn't answer this question, though this was not his immediate preoccupation. The urgency was to get to the village safe with his family. The advancing jungle had reduced the road to a single-track footpath, snaking around growing trees from the centre of the old carriageway, and past vast mudslides and eroding rock falls. Bridges had been washed away, small or big ones, and villagers had managed to line up bundles of mature trees across the old washed away bridges. With bamboos, they had built walls on both sides to help passers-by maintain their balance when crossing, thus preventing them from falling into the water, but some people still found themselves in the water when they tripped. Despite the villagers' efforts, it was impossible to travel all the way along this road without facing water. Such traditionally made bridges were constructed by villagers on some rivers but smaller streams were seen here and there along the path, making people pick their way down to the bottom of the streams' courses and then charge up to the other side. The recent end of the raining season made it harder to walk quickly, because the rain had left holes all over the path, and some fallen trees added to our misery as Father, freshly released from duties, was now marching towards uncertainty.

When the road was in operation, it was hard to walk for a mile without meeting people, but now, we had walked for over three miles without seeing anyone; but at last a figure emerged from afar, with an old bike overloaded with palm wine and food. This person was going to the city. He stopped to greet the family. He had a brief chat with Dad and before he continued he asked, "Are you from here?" "Yes," Dad replied, "but I have not been back for five years, and see what my village has become?"

"You are better here; I have been travelling for three days and want to reach the city to sell my provisions in exchange for soap and oil. We have not seen a car for over two years and we are losing our children and pregnant women as never before! When they are sick, it is difficult to get them to the hospital, and sometimes we carry them through this path; they often die on their way before we reach the town. Some of our sick people prefer to die in peace on their bed rather than attempting this perilous journey. We hoped the independence would bring prosperity and development, but just a few years into it, we now understand that our destiny was not into other people's hands. We understand that things need to be done by ourselves. The new government took power by presenting themselves as the only people who could take this country forward, but clearly it is not the case. Other people who were seen as nationalists were chased, killed and silenced."

"Yes, I know," said Dad; "I am a soldier and have just been sent home. Our job was to silence those rebels and because they have all been killed, I and most of my colleagues have been told that we were no longer needed. Here I am going back to my village I left over 20 years ago, with no hope, no provisions, no indemnity, no plans for resettlement, nothing, apart from these seven children I have been blessed with. What are they going to become and what are they going to eat? If only I could ever reach my village. Let's hope that we gather enough strength to reach the village. This road five years ago was a national road and today, I am walking on a path all the way to my village despite the fact that we have been in charge of this country for just 20 years. At this rate, we will all disappear in 60 years!"

"You are right, we have handed our country into the hands of young turks who have used their flattering language to lure us into believing that our country belongs to us. I am sure they are still serving the colonial power, with the difference that the colonial power can now make our leaders do what they want, from far away. I am sure we are still under the colonial control in some way and that our leaders are nothing other than their servants. It would have been better if they were still here because if they were still here, they would have at least continued to maintain the roads which helped them exploit whatever resources they wanted. Now I am sure, they are still get what they want without any investment in our land to get it, and our ill-trained leaders are busy finding ways to stay in power rather than opening their eyes to the reality. All they want is to preserve the influence that had been handed over to them by the west; after all, weren't they groomed by them"?

"Our true heroes have been killed using stupid people like you. Brothers have been used to divide and kill brothers who have been doing so unconsciously. You thought you were serving your country, but remember that history will tell us who was right and even right now; you can begin to see how foolish we all were. Your chief lured back all those who could oppose them and publicly executed them; now that the country is full of frightened and alienated people, he no longer needs your services. Look, you have been dismissed without notice! People still have the memory of slaughters, the killing of those who dared to stand up against this government. As for me, politics is not the issue, what do ordinary people need apart from peace, food and health? Now apart from the appearance of peace, we are all dying of hunger and diseases. There are no hospitals in many villages and where there are hospitals, they are not properly equipped; hence you have to pay huge sums of money to receive treatment. Over 80% of our people are unemployed and cannot afford any treatment. The so called schools have been created to train another bunch of slaves who are unable to undertake anything by themselves. Once the finish their studies, they sit home and wait for a job. Who will create jobs for them? Before these independences and before the colonial powers, did our ancestors wait for jobs? Did they ever work for someone else? I know and this is what I always tell my children, to create jobs themselves, or rather to invent, create opportunities for themselves because any one who create opportunities is free and those who work for other are servants. It is simple as this. A part from the fact that citizens have been abandoned, our infrastructures have been abused and neglected. Look, just around where we are standing, we have no roads, no infrastructures, nothing! The administration is dysfunctional. There are no rules, no control, and no customer service but a lot of corruptions and nepotism".

"Those who have suddenly found themselves in power are developing a culture of self-help. Yes, we now have a national self-help culture where each civil servant thinks only in terms of personal gain. Bribes, corruption have become the norm in our country. They are helping themselves, not to bring the country forward as they promised, but they are helping themselves to the remains of whatever resources we had left. If everyone follows their example, this country will be sold out in 20 years and you will have to pay to be counted as a citizen of this nation. Yes, I am sure, if they continue like this, there won't be money left to pay them or to maintain their lifestyle, and you will have to pay for every public service. When I think that our hospitals used to be free, the schools were free, I cry when now we are asked to pay for everything to get almost nothing."

By now, the stranger was crying. Tapping his shoulders gently, Dad told him that God would help and that hope was necessary to see tomorrow at this point. The man said, "Let me not keep you too much with these children." He progressed whilst sobbing and coughing.

"May God protect you on your way, thank you and may you have good luck and sell all your produce." It was now getting colder and luckily a group of people were coming from the city, most of them having sold what they had taken and only carrying a few possessions. They greeted us and offered to help. Some of them carried my siblings and helped them with their heavy loads. They were going to the next village, about three miles from Mengan, and they knew Dad. They helped us to the village and offered us some food and beds to sleep in. We spent the night there and continued early the next morning. This was a relief but not surprising. Despite their suffering, they had not yet lost the sense of hospitality and mutual help. Early in the morning we continued with our family and got home around 12 noon. When the road was open, it only took about 30 minutes to cover this distance by car, and two hours walking but today, the journey from my village to new town takes a minimum of 6 hours.

Chapter 2:

The village, like all our villages

It was noon; the sun was over the middle of our heads and each person shadows ringed at their feet, not behind, not long, or very tall. Just there! "It is 12 noon," Mum announced. That is how, in this part of the world, people made sense of where they were and what time it was. The position of the sun and their shadows indicated the approximate time of the day and the sun helped people guess the time of the day until nightfall. At night, it was difficult to tell the time, particularly when the moon was asleep. There were no lights that could be seen at night in the village. It was very dark and trees often seemed like animals or monsters. The quietness of the village at night gave the appearance of a cemetery. Everything was still; quiet and dark only the wind and night birds could trouble this tranquillity.

As soon as we arrived in the village, I noticed that the village houses were hidden beyond the mountains and hills, but they revealed their true colours beneath the green. Yes, it was easy to tell, no matter how hidden it was beneath the trees, that they were all huts. It was pass midday and you could hear the birds singing and continuing to sing their favourite song in this bright sunlit day, even though, for some reasons, no one appeared to care about the beautiful noise they were making. Despite their melodies, everyone ignored or refused to dance to the tune.

Departing from the main path was nothing but a wonder; a different world altogether! Lost in the middle of nowhere, and, not far away, the horizon appeared to mark the end of the world. Some people, I guessed, dared not know or question what was beyond the horizon, yet, beyond the mirage of the close horizon, was another world far way. But the most astonishing thing was that as far as one could walk, the horizon appeared at a similar distance ahead, revealing in between more and more wonders, new trees, new mountains, new forests and, at times, huts and houses that signalled undeniably that people lived around. At times they were those we knew, sometimes those from other beliefs and cultures, but yet in our minds we knew that the land was ours together.

Mengan was small, but happy; yes, a happy village despite the cries of hurt and lack, due to deaths too soon of a child malnourished or a mother in pain, who gave birth in struggle, or the commotions of those who had lost a son or a daughter, without a name yet; the joy long awaited, which soon turned to despair, gripped the hearts of many who had forged the habit of coming together to sympathise, all cried together, to ease their pain. They formed a community of people who had the same history and who grieved together, lived together, suffered in silence, but together they hope of a better tomorrows.

The road in this tiny village, when there had ever been one, or when there was one left, was bumpy and never received the care from anyone who used it, despite the call for works, to make it more alive for everyone to enjoy. The tall trees continued to flourish, canopying the shorter ones, who depended on the mercy of the creator for a little sunlight, and from time to time they became a shelter for the farmers, who after hard work, rested on their feet. On those days, and up to present times, beside the sound of the birds, it was not surprising at all to hear the roaring voices of the chainsaws along the forgotten roads, pulling down the mighty odum and sapele trees of ancient times, just for timber which benefitted not the people of the land, but which was carried away from here, to be used for luxurious household items and furniture, for the pleasure of people known not in this hidden part of the world, forgotten and left alone to fate. If only the beneficiaries could know the true origin of the goods they were enjoying, perhaps they would be human enough to pay the right price or compensation to the land they were so shamelessly robbing.

Descending on the road leading to Mengan, the village where Dad was born, snaked here and there numerous footpaths, branching north, south and forth from house to house and leading to the farms, where livestock were freed to eat and serve themselves on what they could find and judge good enough to eat.

After just a few steps there appeared these small erected structures roofed with dry grasses, sometimes with some rusty iron sheets on them, sheltering human souls from the serpents and scorpions. At night, mosquitoes enjoyed the most, as their duty without fail, from night to night, was to bite. Biting even the eyeballs, digging through the bodies in search of gold and raising the victim's body temperature to a thousand degrees Celsius within a few days; only those with strong will lived. With nothing to slow the mosquitoes' works, most of the time children paid the price with their lives and this explains why there was barely a month without commotions, to cry over the loss of loved ones.

With no pipe-borne water in my village, at day time, little children were found here and there with big buckets and pans heading towards the riverside to fetch water. This river serves as the main source of drinking water as well as water for domestic purposes. Animals, when they had the chance, also bathed, drank and defecated in the same river. After fetching water, children changed jobs, whereby boys picked up cutlass and hoe, and the girls took over their duties in the kitchens.

Education depended on the father's pocket and when more hands were needed on the farm; children born in the farm remained there all the days of their lives.

The dry seasons were accompanied by droughts and bush fires, leading to about six months of hunger and hardship. It was at this time of the year, unfortunately, that we had no choice but to come to live in the village. Like other villages in this part of the world, Mengan was as in the picture painted above. Everyone in the village had a plot of land and lived from the produce of their farm, but what the farm produced was not enough to go on all year long.

Women cultivated the plot whilst men grew coffee and cocoa which was exported to the western hemisphere for chocolate and other delicious products. In this part of the world, people knew each other by name and sometimes organised themselves as a community to help each other.

When Dad arrived in the village, he entered his parents' old house and we were helped by villagers until we were able to fend for ourselves. The villagers knew how generous Dad had been when he was still in the army. Every time he returned to the village during his army's years, he brought them fish, meat, bread, sardines, Maggi cubes and salt. It was now their turn to show their recognition. Villagers truly showed kindess to us. They helped us settle, heped us with farming. In fact, we were well initiated into the village's life and quickly integrated. After a year, we had all forgotten about our previous life in the army barracks. It was as if we had never lived there. Dad blended in easily and was given the title of Chief Counsel. This was in recognition of his experience gained elsewhere during his years in the army as commando. A commando was the name given to unqualified and uneducated soldiers who joined the army to silence the rebellion in the country. He regularly sat on the king's advisory committee.

There was one small school situated in the centre of the village where every young person aged six or above went. I had the impression that some of the pupils were old enough to be my dad. Some left the primary school to get married, both girls and boys. Some girls were getting married to the primary school director or teacher right there in front of our eyes. It was strange for me. Although girls as young as 15 were getting married, must people boys or girls must have been in their early twenties when they left the primary school.

Some children were fortunate to live close to the school, but we were about three miles from the school and we had to endure this journey twice a day as if this was not enough, I will later endure a journey of 18 kilometres every day from Mengan to Sa'a Nzock during my first two years in the secondary school. I was the only child in the village who ensured this fate of 9 kilometres each way to school and back every day for two years.

During our primary school years, we went to school in the morning with our food, spent our lunch break at school and returned every evening. Years went past and the story was being told in the village that Dad helped destroy the rebellion, and for the independence of the country. After peace was affected, he was sent home with his children at the age of 38 with no retirement provisions, no salary and no job. He had spent his youth fighting for his country and helped it gain and ensure stability and peace during the years of independence.

When they were fighting for independence, they had a lot of hope. They hoped that the departure of western countries would give them freedom and growth. They hoped that the change would be effective and that every citizen, now free from the colonisation, would have the possibility to get a decent job. They hoped that the change would bring prosperity and that every citizen would feel it. He was told of a better future for his country, a future that was being undermined and harmed by those who called themselves nationalist. They were being told that if these rebels were nationalists, they would have stopped their fighting and contributed to the development for the country. They were told, and this is true, that it was impossible for their country to progress without peace. Dad was called, like others, brave and intelligent young people to join the army.

He remembers that at his early age, he helped the white men in the road works and in planting coffee and cacao. These were new crops that were being introduced and each person was trained how to grow their own even though no one knew what it was and what to do with it. These plants were being grown at the instruction of the colonial power, for the colonial power. They were mainly for export and food that people needed to eat was neglected.

Using the same techniques he had learned when he was younger, Dad started his own farm and was growing his produce when the war broke out and he was called to defend his country. He was proud to serve this newly formed country and he served for over 20 years in the army. When he was in the army, he was often moved from one village to another and barely had a day off or holidays.

Now back in the village, apart from his farm, Dad worked in other people's farms to earn a bit of money to help him send us to school. Life was very tough; although Mum grew some crops, it was difficult for her to exchange them to get other products, like soap and oil or salt, which were necessary.

Dad often went from village to village to find a bit of work and people often failed to pay him the agreed fee at the end of his labour. There were days he came home covered with blood because he had been fighting to get his salary. He was often mocked as a poor ancient commando who had nothing. He never stopped talking politics. He talked about his disappointment about the government's broken promises and how the country's financial situation had worsened, how they were promised a lot of rewards that had never materialised and how they were sent home like animals without any form of assistance. He talked about his disappointment about the new government cracking down on any person who dares to say the truth, how no one could speak freely, how any voice of opposition was silenced and every political activity prohibited when it wasn't to help the propaganda of the current ruling party. He talked about his delusion of the free and prosperous country that was promised during the independences. What he wanted the most was to see a day when he and his children could have enough to eat.

He had land, but this had been used and re-used by his great-grandfathers and was no longer producing enough food to feed the family. He wished he had fertilisers to help him grow his produce. Fertilisers were available but they were far more expensive than the price of the produce they grew. So my parent worked every day, but we hardly ate every day.

In this forest land, hunger was constant and people wished there was someone to help them with technics to grow their cops better. Everyone was talking about school and this was the new hope of the country. People needed to study in order to get the knowledge required to help the country stand on its feet. What people hoped in the village was that the knowledge acquire at school will help children and the country as a whole discover technics to produce better food, better systems, better tools, great inventions and discover new ways of doing things for the benefit of the country.

Unfortunately, qualifications obtained were those put in place by the colonial power which only trained people to get a job in the administration. People were trained with a servant and jobseekers mentality. At school, people were rather conditioned to depend on other people. People were trained to find a job after their studies. No one was ever trained to become an entrepreneur, all were trained and groomed to become servants and workers in the country's administration. In fact, locals had never been trained to own anything by the colonial power. They were trained to be servants, good servants.

They were trained to get a job in the administration. The colonial power knew why they invented this type of education system. They knew that the administration would hold locals captive all their lives as they worked to gain just enough to eat. Unfortunately, after their departure, no one understood this and no one dared to change the system, worse, it was being maintained and perpetuated.

This was one of the reasons why the country was moving rather backward. There was no new inventions no new ideas, no new technologies, no new machineries, no new industries, no new products made in the country, no new people with new mentalities in our lands. Rather we were still following the colonial system, waiting for the old colonial power to bring new technics, new inventions, new ideas, new technologies, new industries and those industries were in the colonial powers' countries, not in our countries. Few that were in our countries were totally controlled by the colonial power and we dared not to set up ours. You see, we depended on the colonial power for everything including our education and administration system, even though we had chased them out of our land. They were out by still in, and unconsciously they were still controlling and ruling us.

Being the first of seven children, I was the hope of my father. He hoped that if I was able to finish my secondary school, I would get a job and would help him send my brothers to school. He hoped that, if I were able to succeed, there was a chance for my brothers and sisters. He worked hard, borrowed money, sold part of his land; all to push me forward in his limited capacity.

I was brilliant from the start. None of my parents was educated but this was not a handicap for me. Despite my parents' inability to buy me books or to follow me at home, I was able to progress well in class and was always the first of my class during my primary school years. I got my first primary school certificate and started the secondary school, but we knew no one in the city; so I live study in the nearest city while still living in Mengan and for that, I had to troll every day for 18 kilometres, through the bushes from my village to the Sa'a Nzock, the nearest city for my first two year. In my third year, a friend took me in their house and this is how I was saved. I lived in the city for the first time since dad left the army.

I was a brilliant pupil and my teachers put me forward for general studies. I studied biology, maths, French, English,

Spanish, history, geography, citizenship, sport, art, chemistry, physics, philosophy, a bit of economics, but none of these was related to what I could see. Formulae and the names of places were alien; they talk about Trafalgar Square, Waterloo battles, we sang La Marseillaise, talked about the Elysees. These names were foreign and irrelevant to my immediate environment. In geography, I studied the types of climate, vegetation, rocks, mountains, the archaeology, and I knew almost every country and part of the world. In philosophy I studied all the ancients and new thinkers, who were all western thinkers, and was told that the knowledge was universal. In science, I studied the human body, which I understood because I was a human being. In physics, I had no means of testing my theories in the lab and was told that in Europe, students could actually test and see what they were learning. In chemistry, I heard all the names but had no means of trying out what I was being taught, though this would have been useful to me. I was told that there was no money to buy all the equipment needed for a good lesson of chemistry. I learned that a good chemist could find new ways to grow crops, new medication etc. I was also told that most medicines are substances from plants.

I came from the forest and was eager to understand how I could use these plants to cure malaria, and all these diseases that killed people every day. To my disappointment, I completed my A-levels with no expert knowledge in any field. I was told that I could choose to become an expert at the university. I started university, still eager to become a good chemist and help solve my country's food crisis or find a cure for malaria which could help me save lives. I had grown up in a village where child death, hunger and diseases were part of everyday life.

Women were giving birth to as many children as they

could because they did not know how many would survive. My grandmother had given birth 11 times but only my mum survived. In fact, both my parents were the only surviving children of their parents.

The life span was about 40 years and due to the misery, people always looked older than what they actually were. For example, my mum looked older than she was in reality once she returned to the village, after spending years in the city with my dad. In fact, I never remember seeing my parents young. This is odd because I was born when my dad was only 23 and Mum 20, so by the time I started university, my mum was about 39 and my dad 42. They were still young people but their appearances gave them the look of 60 year olds.

During my holidays, I worked hard to get my school fee and books for my younger brothers and sisters. Whenever I had time, I returned to the village to help my parents cultivate the sterile soil from which, despite working the whole year long, we could not eat every day. Having all grown up in the village, people acted as one cohesive and harmonious family.

Though I was taught about races and ethnicities in primary school, this did not mean anything to me until I started university. At the University, I discovered that my ethnic group was said to be the privileged one and others were considered as barbaric. The reason behind this concept was that the colonial arrived in our home town before reaching other parts of the country, and the arrival of these foreigners brought new ways of thinking, new ways of colonising our minds and new ways of teaching us to reject our cultures and we were the first to be alienated. As first assimilated, they paraded and used us as example to subdue others by presenting g us as the best. People to follow and this remained in people's minds and was stocked in unconsciously till then and even now.

They fooled us into signing their treaties quite easily and made us follow them without any resistance. In fact, we were, in reality, their dooms, and the stupid ones, the ones they used to divide and mock others. They used this strategy to overcome any resistance and to dominate others. Using us made it easier to subdue others.

They knew we were not better than our fellow citizens and that we were not necessarily the best, and with hindsight, I understand why they presented us as better people: it is because they were able to manipulate and use us against our own people. For years I was puzzled by this ideology; I have now grasped it, even though at that time what I could remember was my parents' sufferings in the village.

What I could remember was my dad's constant complaints about the new government's broken promises. What I could remember was the hunger people were subjected to in my village. The government which my dad served for over 20 years could not even remember him. How was I from a privileged group when I had to pay my school fees like anyone else? How was I privileged when people were dying in my village and where the one and only hospital served about one million people? How was I more respectable than other people of my country when I barely ate and started taking care of my siblings' age only 13? Did I ever have a good holiday? What would happen to my brothers if I was no longer able to help pay their school fees? Where did this ideology come from? Weren't we all citizens of the same country? I learned to my disappointment that this false ideology was propagated by the colonial power to divide the people in order to have the upper hand on them.

They knew that if they were united, nothing could stop

them. They knew the Bible. They knew the story of the Tower of Babel, when God divided the people in order to prevent them from working together, because by working together, nothing was impossible to them.

My country was now over 20 years into its independence, but nothing seemed to be working. The road left by the colonial had vanished in many parts of the country and those left were quickly degrading and falling into a state of neglect; all the projects that the colonial started before their departure did not continue. New schools, however, were being opened but pupils were being taught the same things, the same system left by the colonial power. Nothing had changed in the education system. Books written by the colonial masters, with names of trees and animals that have never been seen or heard in my country, were still maintained and used, although locals were beginning to write. But even so, their writing did not reflect much our local and national needs.

Our languages had been abandoned and children were forbidden to speak their native languages at school. This was imposed by the coloniser, with a hidden agenda, but our teachers, the master's heirs and servants, continued to maintain the system after the departure of the colonial power, asserting that speaking our native languages hindered our progress in foreign languages.

Did we really need foreign languages? We could have studied using our own languages. It would have been better and we would have understood the deep rooted meanings of words and things. Things appeared to be moving backward. No teacher had re-trained and no techniques were being developed to improve the farming or education system. But the state media said the country was about 80% agricultural. There were few industries in the country and they mainly produced beers and cigarettes tea, coffee and cocoa. Apart from beer being manufactured inland under foreign countries' licences, the tobacco, tea and coffee produced was exported to be transformed in the western world.

The country was producing more and more graduates and the state was the biggest employer. Almost 90% of graduates work in central administration; some of them were recruited as clerks in the cocoa–tea–tobacco farming. These big farms produced enough because they used advanced techniques and chemical products imported from the western hemisphere.

Despite being the richest conglomerates in our country, these farms owned by the colonial masters had subsidies in tax and import on chemical products; yet local farmers who needed help the most were heavily taxed on fertilisers. Yes, it was just unjustifiable to know that there was an agreement in place with the government that allowed these companies to import their chemical product into the country without paying duties, but local farmers not only did not have enough money to purchase such products, but every quantity they managed to buy carried a huge duty fee, which made it difficult for them to sell their produce with profit. The duty fee made it even more inaccessible and unaffordable for locals. Those who managed to buy them could not recover the cost after selling their produce. This inability to break even discouraged willing local investors and people were reduced to using the same old farming methods that had been used for thousands of years. The result was deceiving.

The lack of food to feed the family and the scarcity of money continued to make life very difficult in the villages and small towns. In most village people were subsistence farmers who grew crops at the rears of their houses, and had animals just to feed themselves and their families. Most villages had no schools and the children in these villages ended up subsistence farmers just like their poor parents. The poor farmers had very little to nothing at all from their cocoa and coffee farms because they did not have the money to spray their crops and once the farms became infested, all their hard work just went in vain.

Since most children did not have access to primary education, they became trapped in their various villages all their lives. With the colonial mental programming, they couldn't do much as they thought only through formal education they could better their chances in life. They remained bound because in their minds, they wished they had studied in order to get a job like other. They didn't know that they had a better chance like anyone else to create their own destinies and make of their lives, what they wanted it to be.

Those who managed to escape from the trap of the village into big cities and towns found themselves trapped again in growing slums. Poverty was not something new; it had become part of their lives, attaching itself to their nature like the blood through their veins. It was easy to see it clearly or feel its presence. You could tell immediately when you met such children; some of them appeared emaciated, neglected and sick. The poor were poor and the gap was growing rapidly. Those who were the first into administrative jobs quickly grabbed the state money for their own means, without any consequences.

Those in government were busy trying to protect their power and had put in every key role, people they knew or who had been recommended to them. It was becoming clear that the rich were rich and poor were poor; but, despite all, life was still going on, displaying all levels of poverty in the villages as well as in the cities of our country. There were varieties in cultures and natural resources but a specific culture remained common across all villages and even throughout the whole of Africa.

The culture of poverty and begging and shifting the blame of our own failure onto others was growing; I will talk about this in detail. I will talk about begging, about aid, about shifting the blame. Yes, because this is one of the reasons I studied and I had a solution for this, a promise that I made to myself and to my father, that I will change my country, that I will impact the world and that I will make history. This is my purpose for living, and I promised to embark on this journey of change after my studies.

When I graduated, I found no job even though I never wanted to work for the type of salary that my fellow citizens were receiving. Deep down in my mind, I have never wanted to work for anyone else but for myself. Following what other were doing, I looked for a job after my graduation but everywhere I went, I was asked to give something to get a job.

In almost all official professional tests, one had to bribe to get the job. I did not have money and ended up setting up a small corner shop on the street. Although I was harassed by the tax men who collected the money for themselves, I managed to help my family through this petit commerce. Whilst doing *my petit commerce*, I was still applying to study abroad and was saving in case I was ever offered a place.

One day I received an acceptance letter from one of the European universities. The offer letter was received in early January and without informing my parents, I started preparing myself. I needed a passport but to get one, I was asked to provide all sorts of papers – birth certificate followed by citizenship proof, national identity card, and proof of tax – and each of these documents required not only the official fee, but the bribe fee as well.

It was not a secret for anyone that bribes had to be paid to be served. Sometimes, the bribe was 10 times higher than the official fee and even with the bribe paid, you were never certain to get what you wanted. I was confronted with this sad reality. I spent four months going out every day for my proof of citizenship and national Identity card. I got the Identity card in April and started my application for a passport in May. I paid whatever sum of money I was asked to pay, including the bribe price, which was 10 times the price of the passport. Every day I went to get my passport, I was asked to come back the next day, then next day, then next week and finally they started to ask me to come next month. I complained and filed an official complaint against the officer who took my money; no one ever replied to my letter and the next time I returned to the passport office, I was ushered to the police cell where I spent a week and had to pay another huge bribe to be released. The officer asked me who I was to attempt complaining against him. This was just a little lesson he was giving me as a warning for the future. I understood that there was no point to complain as there was no one to listen to me. Every civil servant was there for themselves, not for citizens and they were all powerful.

Determined to get my passport done, I began a new application in November, six months after the first one, having deferred my starting year at the university. I had to go through the same procedure. I was often told that the passport books were out of stock, the person in charge of signing was off, and so on. I saw people come and go, people were being served, particularly those who knew someone in that department. One day, a man came there for his passport and I decided to speak to him. This person offered to help, and the same day I got my passport even though I was told earlier that morning that there were no passport books. I later discovered that this man was a cousin of the commissioner.

I finally got my passport in June of the following year, seven months after I applied for it and over a year and two months after I first started a demand for a passport.

On obtaining my passport, I put in an application form and got my visa for the United Kingdom in July. I did not tell my family until five days before my departure. Even so, I asked them to keep it secret until I had gone.

We had a small family gathering to celebrate my departing. The joy was at its climax. It was unbelievable that I would be travelling to Europe. I was the second person in the entire county to be travelling abroad. The first person had travelled to another African country and I would be the first to go directly to Europe. Unbelievable! My parents couldn't have afforded the ticket let alone pay my school fees. But through my tenacity and hard work, most importantly through my ability to focus and believe that all things were possible, I had managed to be travelling abroad. I had had this dream since childhood.

In my forest village, I had always dreamed of living in a better place, inventing new ways to work in farms so as to reduce the burden of hard work without results. I dreamed of building a multi storey building with car parks on top. I had never seen that anywhere but I believed it was possible. I dreamed of changing my country and I dreamed of impacting the world. I dreamed of living a better life and I rejected poverty right from my childhood even though I was still living in it, in my mind, I was rich and free. I dreamed of travelling abroad, going to Europe, not only to see some of the places I read about in books, but to learn the best theories and philosophies that I could apply back home to improve my people's living conditions.

When alone in the farm or walking from school, I would be dreaming of my future, representing through my imagination the best conditions possible I would want for myself, my children, my family, and my country. The two years I spent in the road from Mengan to Sa'a Nzock during my first two years in the secondary school were the dreaming and productive years. Every day I would cry, look to the heaven and declare that my condition would change. My conviction that I would travel abroad was so great that I started writing to universities and individuals in Europe when I was doing my A-levels. At times I would apply for bursaries, or enquire about such opportunities. To individuals, I would write for assistance in obtaining visas, for example invitation letters and information on how to get such help. I had a few replies, positive at the time.

One kind family even sent me an invitation letter agreeing to give me free accommodation when I arrived, but I could not afford a passport at that time and if I had managed to have a passport, I wouldn't have managed to pay for the flight ticket, let alone the visa fee. But this reply was an encouragement for me as I knew a time would come when somehow, I would go. Surely this time had finally come and here I was on my way to the United Kingdom.

I had learned a valuable lesson, which was that nothing was impossible to he who believes. I now know that when you want something badly and work at it, somehow, one day, all conditions will come together to make it happen. At that time, I had not had any real contact with the Bible, although I believed in the existence of God; my village had tree-gods or idols and the belief that the dead heard us; that was what I knew even though I didn't practice it. It was later when I became Christian that I understood the biblical principles of what I was doing. That nothing is impossible to He that believes, and doubts not. (Mark 9:23 or Matthew 19:26). I also understood later that all things work together for good to them that love God, to them who are the called according to his purpose as it is written in Romans 8:28.

When the time was ripe, I had what was required for me to travel. The times between my A-levels and Master's Degree and self-employment had been testing times, yet a learning curve where life experience had made me a better person and prepared me for adventure.

Europe was another story altogether.

Once I arrived, I was lonely, crying every day, and knew no one I had ever met in my life. As soon as I arrived, I started to look for a job and a place in other courses at the university but was told that people of my kind had no real chance of securing good jobs. I was advised to apply for cleaning jobs or to work in shops and I was told on many occasions, "This is how it works here." I was not deterred by what people said. When passing one day, I saw people queueing to order in one fast food restaurant. I entered and realised it was McDonald's. Staffs were smartly dressed and I was impressed. I made up my mind to work there and in the same shop. A few days later I walked in and asked to see the manager. The manager came down and I told him I wanted to work in the restaurant. He told me that there was no position available. I went home. Two days later I returned and asked to see the manager again and again he came down and I told him that I wanted to work in McDonald's. He told me again that there were no openings. I returned home again. A week later I was back to the same restaurant and asked to see the manager, who came, and I told him the same thing, I want to work here. He laughed and told me that I had already been there many times and he had already told me that there was no job. I told him that he could do something; he said he could, but only when there is something available. I returned home, two days later I was back again, and this time the manager gave me an application form. I had never completed one in my life and quickly completed the personal information part including my education, mentioning that I had a degree. There was a particular part where they were asking for a reference. I put my previous university lecturer in Africa and my friends' names. Previous work experience I put nothing as I had not, until that point, worked for anyone. There were a lot of questions that I could not answer but I managed to have an interview with the manager, who, at the end, offered me a job. He said that he had to create a position for me and reduce other people's hours and this was down to my enthusiasm and determination. I was sent for training and did not understand a word during the training. They had to make me copy what other people were writing.

My induction was scheduled and I started working just a month after arriving in my host country. At the beginning it was fun, but the days and hours started to appear longer as I calculated how much I was paid per hour. I worked for 10 hours to get £40.

My enthusiasm for working turned to despair when I realised that everyone working with me was either not educated or had dropped out of school or was still studying; but none of them had a degree except the foreigners like me. I left just after three months and moved to another restaurant, where I resigned after two months, and moved to a cleaning job, where I was sacked as I worked very quickly and ran out of things do to and when I did not have anything else to do, I would hide somewhere to sleep or sit somewhere to chat with people. Although my job was well done, I was told that I should always be doing something and that even though I may have finished what I was given, I should continue to pretend working until my time to go off. I became bored.

Despite my earlier success in obtaining a job, when I informed my fellow citizens that I wanted to study and scientific degree at the university, I was advised to opt for what is called vocational courses. I knew I was intelligent and refused to believe. I applied for the course I wanted and was offered an undergraduate place. I enrolled and completed it – not without struggling to cope with the pace of studies and tuition fees.

I immediately enrolled on an MBA course and completed it again but as I couldn't pay my tuition fee, my diplomas were never given; yet I was proud of my achievement. I further studied anything I saw as important to me and my country of origin.

My student years were through. I did all sorts of jobs, when I was given the opportunity; I worked in parking, security, patrolling sites in winter without any heating, or working from one site to the other. I would often cry at night or write my story in books. I would often think about my country, my village and my mother and cry. If only they knew how I was suffering in Europe. This crying time was a crying time. I wrote songs and stories for my book that have never been published.

I could only find relief by believing somehow, miraculously, I would reach the top one day. I thought about how I managed to travel abroad and became fully convinced that I was not stoppable. The only person that could stop me from achieving my dream was myself and the only thing that could hinder my dream was disbelief. I was determined, I would not be defeated. There were days where I walked from bus stop to bus stop, looking for thrown away bus passes to board the bus or train to university as I had no money. When I could find one I would use it and when I was not able to find any, I walked to the university, seven miles twice a day. After all, I had been used to it in my own country and my village.

I went for days at a time without eating and became used to fasting as I would turn my hunger moments to prayer and fasting, praying for a better future and better conditions for myself.

I planned to return one day with my knowledge either to continue my father's dream of a fairer society or to better public services. I thought of no better way to start than by applying for jobs in local government. Without any previous work experience, it was difficult but I knew it was not impossible, so I decided not to give up. After over half of a year trying, I secured my first local government job in the United Kingdom.

Things that my friend who had arrived 10 years earlier than me told me were not possible had started to materialise, and this was down to self-belief and persistence. A key secret I will never forget. I worked and encouraged others like me to apply for similar or better jobs. I set up a training centre offering training to people like me, and the centre became very popular as over 70% of people who received my training secured jobs within local authorities. The income from this job complemented my salary. I started thinking about investing back home. My friend promised to help me and I sent money to buy land. The land was bought, but some people claiming to be the rightful owners built on my land. This was a piece of land that cost me a lot of money. I now started to compare the colonial system of land management against my country's. This is one of the areas I wanted to change when I returned. In fact, I had a hope to see the following areas changed: ensuring citizens security and a fairer and independent judiciary system, reorganisation of the public administration and overcoming of corruption, ensuring land reform and setting up a new land registry system, facilitation of the business start-up process, forging relationships and making our way up, setting up solid training programmes on how to serve our countries, revising aid conditions and moving from spoon-feeding aid to sector-targeted aid, reforming agriculture to fight hunger, assessing the country's and people's needs and catering for them, using people to develop the country and save people and the future, reforming the banking sector and setting up a proper stock exchange, reviving livestock and aquaculture, reorganising the country by regions and counties and setting up county development committees, protecting the environment, ensuring fair trading and price transparency, encouraging regional and sub-regional trades, reviewing and setting up a proper social welfare system, setting up access to healthcare and pension schemes, supporting the elderly and children and protecting the most vulnerable, reorganisation of the insurance sector and setting up a new postal coding and distribution system, and redesigning of new towns, cities, roads, access to water, electricity, ensuring a better refuse collection system, reorganisation of birth, marriage and death register including condition for obtaining citizenship, allowing Public Private Initiatives for road building and railways systems, designing urban transport including inviting private initiatives to fund major transport infrastructures with guarantees for their investment, ensuring the reorganisation of the army, the reorganisation of the country's intelligence system, the reorganisation of the school system and training programmes, ensuring media reforms, setting up regulatory bodies for key sectors and encouraging such in the private sector and, most importantly, build manufacturers in the country to produce what is needed and for export etc. I want the build a new country, a new continent of inventors, trained in the continent.

I want the continent to discover technics and technologies that lift us up and used across the world for the betterment of human being. We can do this without foreign aid and external funding. I would do this using internal resource, or at most, if need be, with the help of the diaspora, but anyone from the diaspora would have to pledge their allegiances to national causes and embrace the country's ideals. This list seemed huge, it looked like I was building a new country from scratch, it was too much and too ambitious a programme; but I believed and still believe I had something to work on. My plan was, and is still, to see what is in this list being implemented before I cross over to eternity. I will give more details on how this will be done.

I had reviewed our long walk from independence to here and realised that nothing had changed. I found out that the situation is even worse because the prison has been transferred to our minds. Our minds have been hijacked, colonised even further, though we are physically free. For me, the euphoria, the hope of independence and a free country with its people had only been an illusion. Nothing had been changed and all these years had ended up yielding less than we had hoped for.

It is only right that we take personal responsibility and become the change we want to see. We talk and want others to do it for us instead of doing the best we can with what we have. The hope that we had then, the hope that our forefathers had had, could be revived through our efforts, provided we refuse to settle for less. Our freedom and true independence is in our hands and it is our duty to take it. We have to discover where the truth lies, and we have to understand that no one is free if his mind is controlled. Therefore, our true freedom and independence should start with our minds. This means ridding ourselves of all subconscious programming of our minds and reprograming them with positive thoughts and self-determination, having a clear mental picture of where we want to be. We need to rule ourselves before we can rule others, we need to be ourselves and to be ourselves, we need to discover our potential, abilities, and our priorities and set up a system that helps us implement values that are necessary for our future generations. It is a shame that, despite our hopes, we settle for less and we still fail to revise our position today.

Chapter 3:

Full of hope but settled for less

Ghana became the first African sub-Saharan country to gain independence from European colonial rule after Sudan, which gained its independence in 1956, but regarded itself as an Arab rather than African country per se. Like Kwame Nkrumah, many subsequent African leaders would serve either as Prime Minister or senior army officer before becoming president. To succeed, all African leaders during the independences sold ideas of hope, fairness, progress, peace and common good, and where there was uprising or serious opposition, young people were called upon to show a sense of nationalism by joining the army in the fight for those ideals. The first governments were elected even though elections may have been made in a way that only the candidates chosen by the colonial won; nonetheless, this was done in a multiparty context. Candidates from different parties fought for elections, but this ideal was soon hijacked by those who suddenly found themselves in power. Here and there in Africa, countries were transformed into one party and oppositions were silenced. At first they justified this with the need for peace and stability, but it was soon discovered that all this was aimed at concentrating the power into the hands of a few, if not one.

Observers soon began to describe the practice of democracy in Africa as 'one-man, one-vote, one-time'. In many of the cases, the winning political party at the independence elections used its majority in the national parliament to pass legislation outlawing the existence of opposition political parties. The ruling party had a monopoly of power and became all powerful. This trend challenged the widely held notion that pure democracy through election leads to more freedom. Those who were somehow elected were progressively redefining democracy in their own way. Conquering and keeping power. They knew Machiavelli for sure. In fact, it was not a democracy and citizens were imposed upon with people to vote for, and they voted under the fear of being singled out.

At the start of, freedom seeking era, as uprisings for independence spread out everywhere in Africa, the USA urged the west for decolonisation with the aim of containing the Soviet Union. The USA wanted some control but could not gain access without decolonisation. The colonial powers wanted to keep absolute control could not resist long enough and had to hand power to a group of unprepared people, or rather, people they had prepared to serve them.

In fact, the colonial power never intended to hand back the power and had only trained a few people in their system, and those who were nearly ready had no long term vision for the country. I doubt if they knew how the country was run. I suspect those in higher positions at that time were no more than clerks and held no real power. This explains why, once in power, they changed.

In my view, there were few educated citizens who had been prepared to serve the country and as they served the master and occupy minor administrative positions. This is because the colonial power never trained people on the basis of the country's needs, nor were they trained to take over and run the country. They were trained to serve them and help them exploit whatever they needed. Therefore, few were prepared for real independence and those who knew what true independence was were vilified, persecuted, killed or forced into exile. Those who were left to lead the country were a bunch of servants that were ready to sing the master's songs, sign any contracts they were asked to sign. They were, however, trained to present themselves as the only leaders able to unite divided countries that were made so to make it easy for the colonial power to rule. In fact, the message of unification will only be on the surface because they will continue in the same principle, tapping into people's egos and culture, presenting some people as barbaric and others as better, based on the language they spoke or how remote they were from the main cities.

Unity and prosperity was sold to Mbii, my father, to entice him to join the army at the time, when the country was in a state of near-permanent rebellion with attempts of secession in some parts of the country. Many citizens were barely at the top of any political position at that time, and with a handful of graduates, many countries, like mine, fell into the hands of turks who suddenly found themselves vying for positions of enormous power and influence, with most of these leaders in their late twenties and early thirties at the time of independence.

Few were in a high position in the army, and those who could convince the west and the USA that they could help maintain stability and keep their interests were placed in leadership positions and given the power through either a sort of election or military coups.

Each person who came to power brought a message of hope and enticed young people to join the army and with their messages of hope, young people who embarked in the army helped neutralise the opposition and countries quickly returned to a central government with only one political party, which was the ruling party. The president's picture hung in every administrative building and most households and people sang his name before the news bulletin and after. Opposition was considered as treason and executions were many. In this context, the United States and its western allies paraded democracy globally as a means to contain communism, but in reality, they embraced autocratic and undemocratic regimes in Africa as long as their interests were served. Equally, western governments' media also turned a blind eye to human rights violations by regimes they supported. In fact, deep within, none of the colonial power really cared about Africa apart from what they were drawing from it.

My father had hoped to serve and live in a free, fair, prosper and democratic country where resources were shared and citizens allowed participating in the political debate. This debate was absent unless it was to sign the glory of the president. My father learned about the extent of the vice when he left the army, unable to feed his family, and with no salary he worked day and night like a donkey just to survive.

In his village, he still had a dream to see what he had fought for become a reality. He still had a dream to live in a country where political debates were not considered a crime, and where citizens were free to speak up for what was right and what they stood for. This was not the case when I was growing up; almost every citizen had a membership card for the ruling party, and every citizen voted, but for only one party. There was only one party and usually one candidate for every election. This even included the legislative or parliamentary because the ruling party chose the candidate for a region and everyone was expected to vote for him. It was also a crime to miss a vote without reasonable cause. Most of the time, people voted without either knowing the candidate's name or why they were voting.

There was never a political programme for every election, even though there was a theme for the electoral campaign. The campaign was just another opportunity for propaganda and self-gratification, to further alienate people and make them venerate and pledge allegiance to the president.

I even voted on behalf of my father a few times when I was still 12 or under. I was allowed to do so provided I presented his voting card, which was signed for at the polling station. It became apparent that one important aspect of the people's and the country's life had been neglected or not even discussed or talked about. Yes, a lot was said about independence, but almost nothing was discussed about the development of the country.

My father, in his mind, expected the independence to bring about development and he wanted to see the continuation of big projects. Hellas! Even now, his village roads are neglected and have vanished due to lack of maintenance and concern from the central and local government.

Everyone in a political position was helping themselves and they still do. Democracy was the right to vote, and to vote for the person you have been asked or imposed to vote for in the context of one unique political party; so was democracy redefined in Africa. It is true that nowhere had democracy been a situation where the majority holds power. The minority had always held power, through alienation and bribery of the majority. The majority are ignorant and dance and play the game in which they are always losers, but at least the rules are accepted elsewhere than Africa. Citizens were fooled in this way and made to believe that they were participating in a democratic process. Many of our politicians were showmen who disguised the corrosive effect of their rule on the country's sense of order and justice.

Our way of rendering justice was neglected, but what we embraced was worse. Even though African countries had their own legal systems which worked before the colonisation, this was abandoned and the chief's power was erode and taken away by the colonial powers to the point that there was no longer a counterbalanced of power for those who ruled; abuses started from the head down, from top down.

We neglected both our systems and the colonial power's, but our newly over-empowered leaders undid these systems creating a sense of anarchy and self-help, where those in a position of power could act as they wished with impunity and without being brought to account or to justice; and, where justice was possible, they created a system of corruption to pervert the course of justice, thus ensuring that they were never prosecuted. Africans became expert in national self-help and impunity. They knew and know how to draw the best from the public services to their own advantage and western companies loved it because the chaos helped them to exploit as much as they could. After all, those who commit sin with you will soon commit sin against you and you will have no authority and courage to challenge them. They are mimicking what you normally do together.

Many African leaders considered themselves as friends of foreign western nations and they were in between the eastern bloc and the western. Even so, the poverty in which citizens were living did not make them think about a long term development plan for the country.

They did not do anything to help their people have

enough food to eat, and the only thing they seemed to have encouraged was studying with school programmes copied from the western model, but never adapted it to their country's needs or cultures. The models of development or planning for the country's future or needs would have been good examples to copy. The land registry systems and democracy, amongst others, would have been good to copy, but no. This was overlooked. There were good things to be copied. For example, the communists ensured that their people had enough food to eat. The former colonial powers ensured that there was enough food available in their own country and set up welfare systems to alleviate the burden of poverty among the poorest. This was not perfect, but it ensured that the less fortunate were looked after. These are other examples we should have copied, but we did not.

In reality, we expected much and received nothing from our common resources that were hijacked and monopolised by those who fooled us to work for them and who sold the illusion that our happiness depended on them. We ended up with almost nothing! Our children, brothers and sisters died for nothing, almost nothing. It was better not to make us dream, it was better to let us have a dream of our own, not a common dream that never materialises. It was better not to make any promises; after all, we would have acted expecting nothing in return. It was better, yes, better to take more time to prepare ourselves and plan before taking over. Yes, I am controversial but delaying a bit would have been better. Oh, I forgot, we can't stop history, but at least once we were in, we should have stopped and questioned the very reasons that justified our fight and quest for independence. Why did we fight so much for independence if we were going to come out worse losers? Why did we have to lose lives if we were not going to change nothing? Why did we bother chasing the colonial power away if we were going to continue to serve them in a disguised way?

It was time, then, to go through this stage. Of course it is a lesson, and we are learning. Learning about our miscalculations; learning about our mistakes, yes; at least, if only we could learn.

Many big programmes were initiated with indebtedness and the vision was for a short time. Money was borrowed to fund vanity projects and empty promises were made of the future. Promises that rested on nothing but hope and wishes! We wanted to be self-ruling but counted on others to support us even though we had everything at our disposal to do it by ourselves. Yes, we were ill prepared but once we had the opportunity, we could have learned and studied hard to know what should have been our priorities. We didn't, and went with the wind and left ourselves to chance, and we were carried out of our comfort zone to the point that we became strangers in our own land.

People had to tell us what we had in the countries, how to exploit and use it and who would use it and what, if we were lucky, we could get as leftovers; and we had no choice but to accept it as they imposed on us. We soon started to cry and complain that we were still not free even though true freedom had never been given. True freedom is knowledge, the knowledge of the truth. If we knew the truth, it would have set us free but we cared less to search for the truth, so we failed to discover the truth and as a result, we remained imprisoned in our own minds.

In the words of Plato, we were and probably still are in the cave where we fail to perceive the true form of things. Appearances are never the reality. Official discourses are never the true reason why things are said. Behind every official theory was the real world, and this was the truth that needed to be discovered and this has never been given to anyone, they each person has to discover it. Knowledge and freedom is a voyage of discovery and self-discovery.

Plato's allegory of the cave and understanding reality is an example. Plato believed that as well as the transitory material world that we all experience here and now, there is also an eternal world of concepts or forms. This eternal world for Plato is more real than the world we experience through the senses, and it is the object of knowledge, not opinion. Plato believed that the material world cannot reveal the truth, or rather, that the official discourses are fake because they can only present appearances, which lead us to form opinions, rather than knowledge.

The truth is to be found elsewhere, on a different plane, in the non-material world of ideas or forms. For Plato, in order for something to be real, it had to be permanent and unchanging. We can see why yesterday we had the sensation and feeling of being free when we chased the colonial power away, but soon after they left physically, we started running after them again so they could come and that what we chased them away for. We asked them to leave because they were exploiting our resources for themselves and ruling us without our consent, but just as they went, we ran after them against begging them to come and exploit more of our resources and this time, they imposed on us, more drastic conditions that holds us more captive than before.

This was evident and inevitable because the systems they had set up did not allow us to be free without changing them. We would have been free by now if we had changed the colonial systems at an earlier stage of our independences. We would have found our way around and we would be ourselves by now if we had taken time to identify our strengths, our abilities and potential and find internal solutions to solve our problems.

The solution is never far from where the problem started. Selling petrol and gold to others will never set us free. We will only become free when we know what to do with our petrol and gold, mines, cocoa, coffee and find our own way of realising their potential. Value added has never been found in a commodity in its natural form. The value is created when the commodity has been transformed, ready to be used. This is the rule for every commodity. Potatoes fresh from a farm will always cost less than fries. Petrol fresh from the well will always cost less than its derivatives. This is because during the process, their value has been added through stages of processes and transformation. So what can I say about gold, diamond, uranium, cobalt, zinc or petrol? We want to add value to these natural resources and reap the benefits, let's transform them in our land, or else, let's preserve it. If they colonial power want them so much, let us become equal partners in the transformation process and let's set up, here in Africa, factories to transform its derivatives, which are even more precious.

Our problem is that we chose to maintain their system; it is only normal for us to remain bound. We are playing in someone else's terms not ours. This is the principle of the battle of forms. So our principle must be spoken out, our priorities clear and our will dictate when it comes to what is important to us. We must first be confident that we are free before expressing it.

Our concept of liberty and independence was the product of opinion, not that we knew the true meaning of independence and freedom. They rest not outside of us, but inside. Our mind only can set us free, not a man or a powerful nation. But instead of turning within to find a solution, we turned without and that is why our expectations were cut short. This is still the reason why we haven't found our place in the world and more reason why the struggle continues.

When we hear that a nation has become wealthier, we rush to them and invite them to come to our country with nothing tangible to offer, we offer our natural resources, even those that have not yet been discovered, and we sell them with our future generations to meet our needs of now, caring not about the future. We are selling to China today and in 30 years' time we will be the ones complaining that China had fooled us. Of course they are fooling us. They wouldn't have paid a penny if they were not maximising in terms of profit. They are serving their interest like others did. They will exploit and inundate our land with what they have for now to grow their economy and country, and I would not be surprised if it comes to a point where they sit at the table with the former colonial powers and the United States of America like the west did in Berlin to share our land without us again. Africa was distributed, shared in their absence, far away in Berlin without African people's consent or knowledge.

We knew that before the independences and we didn't think well before they left. We were full of hope when we chased the colonial power away, and we are still full of hope when we bring other vultures like China in and they all come for the same reasons, grabbing the best we have, as fast as they can, taking the best they can take; and this will continue as long as we continue to dream that another nation will help us to develop. Why would they? They are in the surviving business and if they need us to survive, they will use us as long as they can. At the centre, it is not us but themselves that they are serving; it is not our interests but theirs that they are trying to preserve.

Yesterday, we accused others of using us and we prayed

for a better tomorrow where we wouldn't be lured into selling our resources cheaply. It was a simple wish without plan or strategy and, as a matter of fact, we are still making the same mistakes today, and the tomorrow we were praying for is already here and now; yet without questioning ourselves, we are praying again for another tomorrow, without planning. We have prayed without actions; it is now time to act with faith and stop living day by day, planning from month to month to the point that when we are unable to pay our public sector workers, we borrow to pay our debt.

With economists and intellectuals in our governments, we do not stop to think that it is a bad practice to borrow to pay our debts. As long as we continue to do so, we will never overcome indebtedness. We can borrow to invest, not to pay debts, as by so doing we pay interest twice. Surely this practice of over-reliance on debts to finance our debts leads to auto bounding. What did we hope for? Perhaps for a better future! But how did we negotiate our way out of these chains?

Even though we had the upper hand then, I mean a the time of independence, with our resources that could not be found elsewhere or easily substituted, we still negotiated on bad terms; so was it also with our independences. We negotiated on bad terms because we had no strategies. If we had good strategies, we would have been better off because at the time of our independences, the colonial power was fighting on many front and as result, they were weakened. If we had collectively negotiated better terms, we would have won. Let's remember that they would have had no choice but to let go. Since they were fighting in many countries, they would have crippled themselves if they had chosen not to let go.

We missed the opportunity to negotiate better deals. I

guess because we did not consider ourselves equals as a result of what was programmed in our minds- as we were programmed to think as inferiors. Yes, our immediate bosses, who made us who we were, sat at the table with us to make an offer. We did not reject it because we were concerned about ourselves rather than our common good. We lost the mind's tactics, the only weapon we had at our disposal. What about today? We sign every conventions, every treaty that binds us to terms that all play in our disfavour, and so, we sign treaties against ourselves, thus selling our children's rights to stand for what is right for their times all for copper pennies.

It's never too late and we are on our way back, we will emerge and stand, if new weapons manufactured and given to our own foolish brothers don't finish us. Sophisticated weapons are seen here and there in the desert in the hands of those we officially call terrorists, yet we can't explain where they bought them from, though the mark reveals their makers. They - the world police- stay silent and leave us to our fate. How do these terrorists communicate? Where do they hide when today we can see and hear people in their bedrooms? This is not my purpose.

We expected freedom and a better life, which can come from no one else but ourselves. If we want it, we can have it, through effort of ours, drawing from within and not without. But we can't overcome these limitations without understanding how we acquired them. We cannot free ourselves if we don't know how we became enslaved. We cannot liberate ourselves without understanding how our minds were programmed to think the way we do now. This, again, is to say that the truth is never what we see at first glance. The truth is always hidden, ready to unveil itself to those who seek it. This means that we need to train our minds to investigate with care in order to uncover what had been programmed in our minds, and how to overcome it.

Descartes wouldn't have discovered his principles of truth without doubting that what he had received till then through his education was questionable. In my view, our minds were programmed through education, the education system that was introduced in our countries, and it continues to influence our way of life.

Education plays a part in what we are and only through a process of re-education can we change for the better. If we have been fed with limitation, fears and doubts, only through a process of re-education can we change and reverse this situation. We can therefore confirm that education, though good because it gives us a sense of direction, can also limit us when it has been carefully designed to work this way, and as we grow, we become even more restrained.

A young child has a blank mind and can do, if he imagines, what he wants, so has it been said and proven. It is only normal to act like servants if we have been trained to be servants. Equally, if we are retrained as winners and masters, we will start acting like masters and winners. This is the type of education that we need. We now need to train our children to act and behave like inventors, creators, winners, researchers, able people who can discover with a can-do mentality.

Our mechanics need to know that we are looking forward for new engines, new cars, new machines, and they are the only people who can bring us these inventions as their brain child. Our researchers need to know that malaria will be defeated only if they can find the cure; our doctors need to know that we await for the solution from them for these diseases that hinder our progress and bind us.

Our teachers need to know that our children are to be trained as solution bringers to our needs, not as beggars, so they should instil in them the winners' mentality. They should infiltrate in their minds, this ideas that they are the best and inventors, creators, promoters and world changers of tomorrow; our public sectors workers needs to know that we expected so much from them, to deliver first class services to our citizens with efficiency and effectivity. Our farmers need to know that we are waiting for them to produce enough to feed our people and that new techniques are core to doing this, and therefore, along with our researchers, they have to work together to solve our food crisis and underproduction problems. We need to put an end to food importation; our lands are fertile and can produce more than we need. We need to change our mind-set, moving from the servanthood mind to mastermind thinking. True we have been trained as servants, it is time to rid ourselves of this demining thinking and act as men and women of valour. We wanted our independence because we wanted our self-determination. Let us prove it, that we are able to do better than what people thought we could do, that we are free humans like anyone else anywhere in the world. See how we were trained, to serve and to be servants; is it what we want to maintain? I am sure not. Let's expose and dismantle this old system once and for all. To all Africans who believe all things are possible, to all those who love Africa, your unconditional love will not go to waste, as long as you continue to believe that change is possible.

Chapter 4:

Trained to be servants

Our spiritual conditions determine our material conditions and I stand against those who believe that our material conditions will determine our living conditions. Nothing has ever been brought into being without starting as an idea in someone's mind. Therefore everything we think we can make for sure can come to light, if we will it enough to call it as we wish to see it, and focus on how to bring it to the fore. Equally, anything we think we can do, we are also able to do. To start the process of materialising our idea, we need to have as much details as we can in our mind to speed up the process, and our tongue is a key, because words have creative power in a sense that what we say always comes to pass.

We need to call what is yet unseen as though it was here now, and the more we do, we will see it in reality. We shouldn't worry about how we will get there because this is the barrier that puts the fear in our heart and limits the power we have. Everything was created by decree. Everything that was created was through the use of words, either pronounced or materialised, as I bring you to agree with me that words are ideas, and as simple as it sounds, it remains the key to the achievement of all we need and want.

Because our mind is so powerful, if something goes through our minds, it will change our actions and alter our way of life. Those who understood the principle of words and education set up systems that helped them to achieve their expected end. The colonial power knew that they could not get through to African people and change their way of life without changing their thought process and this is why they devised several methods to reach their goals and the education system was one of the powerful tools they used.

The colonial education system became a building field for slow motion bombs that is now playing against African people, thus serving those who programmed their minds in this way. When people are constantly told they are inferior, they end up believing and accepting it as a truth; if people are constantly exposed to these lies, particularly when they are told that they have been sold like any other commodities, it will be hard for them to reject other lies that are filtered through their minds without a very strong will power. Though slavery had taken place in every continent with every race, African's slave trade was particularly humiliating and continues to be a tool to diminish and demise Africans. If perpetrators can officially acknowledge it as a crime, pay for and repair the damages, we will be rehabilitated and this will give us confidence that, to a certain extent, the perpetrators have remorse and recognition that we Africans are equals. We shouldn't shy away from this fundamental demand and I herewith send a formal request to the perpetrators for reparation of damages. If slave masters were paid over 67 billion pounds sterling as compensation to stop their trade, slaves and those who suffered from slavery should even have more compensation. The continent was drained from his able people and many died as result, yet this has never been considered as crime against humanity, what a shameless behaviour!

Germany paid for the occupation of countries and is still settling economical damage to those countries that they occupied during the world war two. Slavery was not only humanely shameful, it was also economically damaging for the African continent and the perpetrators' refusal to pay for the damage and to apologise shows how little they care about Africans as fellow human beings.

Slavery drained Africa from our able, healthy, hardworking and to a certain extent, best brains. Our lands were emptied to build another land, and we are not even recognised as builders or contributors to the building of these nations. The refusal of the west and the USA to repair the damages also highlights their lack of consideration and respect for a whole African continent. It is their way of saying "what can you do?" This is my view; their refusal to apologise for this atrocity shows how little the perpetrators care less for what we think.

Slaves built the USA and western economies, it is as simple as that and damages need to be quantified and paid for. This money could be paid directly to the African Union or to countries that suffered the loss. In Fact there was no country in Africa at the time and some people who find themselves far away in the remote places of Africa where slavery never took place where probably running away to hide as result losing family members. When we look at these historical unacceptable realities, we understand why education was later used as a weapon against Africans.

Equally, after the slavery, we suffered another blow of imperialism where our land was occupied against our will; kings and queens were killed and deposed, our cultures were ramshackle, our traditions distorted, our history falsified and our museums stolen. This was not only an act of aggression, but it is internationally not acceptable. In today terms, it was a crime against humanity. Let's hold someone to account.

Germany paid for occupying some countries during the war, yet our land was occupied for years and years, during which time our cultures and social fabric were destroyed. We need adequate compensation for this I continue to ask.

We were told education was for our own good. It is true that on the surface everyone agrees that education is good; it is the type of education that was programmed in our subconscious mind that was not good. For example, if children are educated to become radicals or terrorists, no one will accept it as they will surely graduate as terrorists, but if this type of teaching is made official, it is clear that the outcome will be to produce radicalism. Similarly if we are trained to consider ourselves as inferiors, the outcome will be the production of inferior people; if we are trained as servants, we graduate as servants; if we are trained as beggars, we graduate as beggars and we were certainly trained to be beggars, servants and inferiors. This is why we consider ourselves as inferior and dependents and these are the signs that we show everywhere we go and in everything we do. Inferiority complex and begging spirit are the character that we exhibit in our interaction with the West. We do this unconsciously because we have been programmed to act alike. Only through an act of consciousness, pride, rejection of stereotypes and preconceived ideas can we destroy these barriers. When we start having confidence in ourselves as human beings who first transformed the world through our great civilisations, we will regain our place in the world.

The outcome of our colonial education system is evident; we act and do like servants, inferiors and dependents. Even though we have managed to take physical control of our nations, we are still psychologically dependent on the colonial power, counting and relying on the colonial power for most of the things we do. This again is because they had programmed our mind to respond in this way; and, by doing and by acting in this way, we continue to serve them as well as their interests. They continue to impose and dictate what should or shouldn't be done in our countries. They continue to determine resources that should be exploited, when they should be exploited and how, and who should exploit them. We do so even unconsciously because this has been programmed in our subconscious mind I say it again. I am far from denying the importance of education. In fact education is crucial to impose an ideology as much as it is central in training able people who can think critically and solve problems. But, only when we start to review and rid ourselves of lies as well as official discourses imposed upon us by the colonial powers during their years of occupation and beyond, through various networks, structures and communication channels that we will truly be free.

Through our ability to rid ourselves of myths, culture and official discourses which tend to favour the systems put in place, we become free and can easily pinpoint underlying lies that have infiltrated our minds. This is not an easy task and few people dare to detach themselves from this pack of lies programmed in their subconscious mind.

Whether we accept it or not, I maintain that gently, subtly, systematically, surely and slowly a conscious programming of our minds was implemented and established throughout the years of colonisation, forgetting no details and using all means, such as: force, intimidations, slavery, forced labour, educational system, media, books and ideologies, race and colour and racial tactics and arguments, aid and pity, bullying, division, mockeries, diplomacy and sympathy, bilateral agreements, fake and biased researches, colonisation and imperialism, doctrines and sects, technology and currency, trade and customs, taxes and duties, medicine and government systems, coalition, fraud and theft and all sorts of media. Yes, theft; theft is not just taking forcefully using physical or disguised plans, stealing is also using mental manipulation to get something that is not ours, which otherwise wouldn't have been obtained. Fraud is also using ruse or manipulation to cause financial loss to someone whiles making gain from the third party's losses. In simple terms, we fake things to make you lose whilst we gain from your loss. This is fraud and Africa has certainly suffered a great deal in the hands of the western powers during colonisation and beyond. We have been victims of all this. We are still victims of all this and it has been made in the way that we barely understand or question it.

The package had been well designed, well presented and subtly programmed in our unconscious and subconscious minds. Nothing has been spared to achieve the goal. Now, we do, act, accept, and live the way we are expected to do. I cry every day seeing how Africa and Africans are portrayed on TV programmes. Only misery and suffering, people eating dung and we, leaders of Africa, are happy, because this is shown so we can collect donations and aid. This is rather shameful and further builds a culture of inferiority vis-à-vis Africa.

The hands that give are always above those that receive; clearly, being at the receiving end, we are under giving hands. This is not structurally what should have been in reality. It is that through conditioning, we have been disabled to act, think and find solutions within ourselves to respond to challenges we face. Since we cannot provide for ourselves, we have been told that there are able people who care for us and who can help us overcome our suffering and misery. We accept these lies as result of our mental and physical laziness, and opt for an easy option. Begging! Yet we know that our freedom and salvation cannot come from anyone else than ourselves.

All our endeavours should have been focussed on self-liberation, self-improvement. Our education system should have been key to training able minds, and to ensure our citizens receive specialised knowledge. Unfortunately it is not the case. We train people in everything but who are good in nothing in particular. Our engineers know a bit of everything, but nothing properly, this helps us to get by using what other people have invented.

Look, I was trained in Africa, starting with the education system that was bullying, intimidating and full of things to learn. In some classes we studied up to 23 subjects and did exams in all the 23 subjects. Why study so many things? Do we really need all of these subjects? No, we need specialised knowledge not general knowledge that leads to vague application of learning. Our systems lead to confusion instead and the west left this system because they wanted people who would run when they whistled. They wanted people who do a bit of this and that without being good at anything in particular. They knew it and they used it to insult us when they called us "bon à rien" in French –, "good in nothing" – and we continue to train the good-in-nothing children. Our system favours classroom achievement, heads full without specialisation in anything. There was never a focus on outcomes and what we would become at the end of our studies or what we could do in life. The focus was and is still on success, achieving high grades and amassing diplomas. I finished school without ever knowing what I could become and no one discussed this with us. Jobs are mostly in public administration and to some degree in the banking sector, a sector that collects people's money, and uses it to pay their staff. African banks rarely create any values because the system has not been design to help to thrive. It is difficult to get a secure loan because Most African's land registry system is extremely inefficient. The bullying, intimidation and focus on completing education and having qualifications was inherited from the colonial power. People know that when you have diplomas, you stand a chance of getting a job. Yet, qualification does not guarantee fitness to practise and does not confer the skill set to perform at the expected level. This system has failed us, yet no one is changing it.

Comparing the European educational system with African system, I note a good difference. In Europe and other so-called developed countries children are trained to have self-esteem, confidence and to discover their abilities, which in turn help them to discover their true purpose in life. No one can go wrong if they are operating in their area of calling and purpose.

No single person was created to fail, but success can only be achieved when one works in their purpose. Children in Europe and other western countries are trained to respect others, starting with simple things like waiting your turn, acting orderly, for example like queueing, but in contrast, our bullying culture raises people who want to do to others what they were subjected to. It is who is stronger that wins and imposes upon others. Children who are bullied tend to be bullies themselves. In public services, without respect for others, a man will just come and jump the queue to get what he wants; if he is confronted, he will bully and ask others complainants to challenge them if they can, and so it goes.

No one respects the other, and this is replicated in the delivery of public services, hospitals and all sectors. Those who are stronger take control by force, not through a consensus, and the leaders become the dictators, because they are leaders not by consensus, but by force. Any leader who takes position by force will not tolerate challenges and will also kill creativity in others people, who prefer to preserve themselves and the privilege they hold for that moment rather than lose it, as they know from experience that nothing would change if they were to leave.

This is programming; our forefathers saw our lands being taken by force and their leaders, kings and queens being killed by the colonial and imperial power that took over by intimidation and bullying. Brothers and sisters were bullied, brutalised, humiliated and even killed in public and in public services during colonial rules, school children were bullied, mocked and ridiculed during lessons. One day, the perpetrators were gone, leaving the space for those who learned and worked under them. As servant trainees, they were used to bullying and mockeries, so when they took over, the only effective methods they knew was bullying and mockery as well as the use of force to make others follow them. They carried on perpetrating the same system, completely ignoring their annihilating consequences. This extends to every area and key sector in our society, where unconsciously this was maintained as we knew not the alternative. Even up to now, we behave as if everything that comes from the west is good; so we were told and so we believe, we were forced to accept it in this way, because we were called barbaric, uncivilised. Why do we continue to accept it today then? It is because the conditioning is acting through our unconscious mind.

Africans people were told that others nations, particularly the colonial power came to teach them a better way of life. This was not hidden, it was a clear programme and they signed up to it, willingly or forcefully, and over a period of a hundred years and more. So children were born in this system, they were taught to accept things as they were, they grew up transmitting the same false information to their children and, as a result, a whole generation of fooled individuals is groomed, raised to serve a system that profits them not, in total ignorance.

Besides this theoretical manipulating system, our minds had been hijacked. We even question this system sometimes, but quickly settle for what we see as comfortable. After all, laziness is spiritual and the fight need to engage should be rather spiritual, more spiritual than physical. Most people think that we should fight again to gain total independence; this is a bit naïve because we have no heavy guns, no mighty army, no missiles, and no nuclear weapons. We should never engage in a physical battle, since guns, missiles and machines will help to defeat us, but if we will, we can overcome through our mental strength, tactics and well planned strategies.

I have identified that some of the methods used by the colonial power to submit Africans have been obvious, and others apparent, but many unnoticeable. The obvious ones we will not dwell on, for example war, force, forced labour, slavery etc. The most subtle methods have been pity, aid, mockery, sympathy, multilateral agreement, treatises.

But one may ask, how have mockeries been used to submit us unconsciously? I have discussed this earlier but for now, I go to the point, when people point to Africans people's nose, and mock it, when I they were bullied because their nose is large, when people conclude that they had no language or that their language, their culture were barbaric, or that my social organisation is nonexistent, how does this make them feel? Is it not what the colonisers used to dominate Africans further and is this still not in practice today?

One may ask, how have mockeries been used to subjugate African people unconsciously? I have discussed this earlier but for now, I point to the nose, the language, the culture, the social organisation. Haven't we been told African cultures were barbaric? Yet did they invent the guillotine? Did they invent auto-da-fe? Yet we accept that we may have been barbaric. Haven't we been told African languages sounds bizarre? Have you heard Chinese, Welsh and German? They can't pronounce Mbamga but can pronounce smurknowivk, they can't pronounce Ndzie but we can pronounce Umweltverschmutzun or Brustwarz without difficulty, and so on and so on. Another may ask, what has sympathy or pity to do with this? I reply, when you tell us how you cry for the loss of my children, when you point to the sleeping sickness and hide behind it to justify why I can't develop livestock, in a green pasture of my land, just because you know this is an easy thing I can do to earn money without too much sweat. Tell me, was sleeping sickness the real reason why in central Africa livestock were not encouraged? I am sure not, it was a plan to prevent people from entering this sector that would have facilitated their economic freedom.

You come to mourn with Africans because kids are dying, whilst trying to sell new medicines, new vaccines or selling them at odd prices in credit to make them bathe in debts for life and because you are with them in crying, they cannot complain or question the real reasons behind your help. You constantly pity them and tell them that the only solution is for you to give them something to eat and by so doing you keep them where they are, so you can control them better. Through your aid programme,

African people's minds and mental abilities to find solutions to their problems have been disabled. You have enslaved them with aid and now, you can buy whatever they have at the price fixed by yourself like it was some sort of favour you were doing them. You need them, but you pretend they were the one who needed you. You need them more than Africa needs you. You need Africa more than they need you. Without Africa, you wouldn't be a great continent and your industries wouldn't exist, because you will have nothing to power them. You, the coloniser came to Africa first because you needed what Africa had, and when they resisted you came out with all sorts of strategies to get it anyway. This is why, at any given time, you have made them adopt all sorts of programmes in almost every area of life, to distract and keep them busy, and their mind in this way is being programmed to look up to you and depend on you.

And the programming was subtle and gentle! You brought schools and I said that school were good, we know that education is good, and so schools were put in place to teach Africans how to serve the colonial power. They were training people how to serve their country but in reality, they were ruling the country and de facto, they were training people how to serve them. All systems were tailored to their needs, not to African people's needs.

In reality, African people were trained how to serve the master. They wanted people to be loyal Loyalty, fidelity, to whom...? And so little by little, they drank the lies, accepted truncated facts, false ideologies and fake realities until they became the norms of life.

Our thoughts and actions are continually being guided by the subconscious mind, and the programming within makes us act in a certain way. Therefore failure and despair, success as well as positive thinking or self-belief are its products. The more we hear certain things, the more they infiltrate our subconscious minds and the more they infiltrate our minds, the easier they become believable and accepted as truths.

We African people see ourselves as free agents yet deep beneath, we are still attached to the colonisers. We serve them at will without realising the causes behind the way we act. We are free in flesh, but tied in minds, yet the mind without the will responds to how it was trained to act. That is why I say that we are physically free but still emotionally, psychologically and mentally assimilated.

We are in reality enslaved on our own accord without even realising it and this behaviour pattern has been passed down to us through soft and subtle systems. The type of education system we received was obviously one of the main vehicles for this and we dare not change it, thereby accepting and continuing the same system that holds us down. Until we are mentally emancipated and free, until we are psychologically and spiritually free, and until we believe that we are free, we will never be free. We read books, attend universities, and study authors like Pavlov but apply none of their theories to improve our continent, and as a result we remain bound and annihilated. We freed our land but remained mentally linked to the colonisers using their systems that incapacitated our minds.

We have been conditioned in Pavlov's way, and even free we still behave as subjects. Pavlov proved with dogs that a conditioning repeated for a certain period will become a habit that if not change, will determine our future conduct, guiding one's actions and behaviour. With Pavlov, a dog was put somewhere and every time a bell rang it was given food and after this experience was repeated several times, the dog began to salivate each time a bells rang. The Dog has started to associate the bells with food. The dogs learned to associate the sound of the bell with food to the point that without food, the sound of the bells triggered the same response.

This experience has also been done with a big cat that was put in a big glass house. Each time it tried to move, it hit its head on the clear glass to the point that the cat became used to the confinement and one day, the door was opened but it did not dare move beyond where it was used to staying, because in its mind, the barrier was still in place. With all respect to ourselves, I think we been fooled alike. It is up to each of us to judge.

But anyhow, the theory is clear, that a change in behaviour can be triggered by training or education. As we can see, our behaviour can be conditioned by the way we are taught, trained, initiated or contained. Can we African really say that our education, Administrative system, trade patterns, reflects our inner way of thinking? Where did we copy the way we act today? Can we change it? I think yes we can change it. We can be ourselves if we want.

Watson summarises the impact of conditioning in the following words: *"Give me a dozen healthy infants, well-formed, and my own specified world to bring them up in and I'll guarantee to take any one at random and train him to become any type of specialist I might select – doctor, lawyer, artist, merchant-chief and, yes, even beggar-man and thief, regardless of his talents, penchants, tendencies, abilities, vocations and the race of his ancestors."* *(John B Watson, 1924, p. 104)*. I therefore conclude that our current way of thinking is the legacy of the colonial power.

The colonial subconscious is our brake and it is still at work. We were trained to serve and conditioned to perpetuate servantship and display a subordinate's behaviour. We were never trained to create or to own anything, we were trained to get a job, not to research and

and create. This is why most of our businessmen are those who never studied in the colonial system. In Cameroon, we have the like of Fotso, Kadji in Burkina Faso we had the like of Kanazoe, they had no inferiority complex and no excuses, they were just themselves and lived to their purpose. There were never labs or extensive research centres to equip future generations. Most of our jobs were meant to be in the area of public administration and teaching. These sectors don't create anything. They train people to perpetuate the system.

Some may argue that we are not acting like servants and that we have not only been trained to serve. I maintain that this is the case. Our minds have been poisoned and disabled and the poison injected in our subconscious affect the way we see ourselves and the way we think about ourselves. We think that we can only do better if we have the west with us, we think that our discoveries can only be validated by the west, we think that our diseases can only be cured by the west or that good medicines and vaccines can only be discovered in the west. We make discoveries, instead of using them to advance, we want to convince the west to accept it and they surely denigrate it, and once they have done so, we abandon our projects as if they were useless. Yes we may have got it wrong at the first instance, but we can improve on what we have already discovered. We don't need anyone validation of ourselves. We are people, different, independent, able equal in nature.

Let's overcome the message of lies and deceit that has been programmed in our subconscious in forcing our way of life to become the production and reproduction of the deceptive programming received for nearly a century. TV programmes, radio, writings or teaching are aimed to programme us in a certain way. Yet it is undeniable that our only weapon for freedom is our minds. Just as we have been programmed through our minds, our way out will be through a mental reprogramming of positive though and the development of can do and self-belief mentality. Yes, our conscious tells us that we are not free, our subconscious tells us that we can't do anything as we will not be allowed. our natural mind confirms our freedom, and the Holy Spirit in us bears witness to our freedom.

This complex that had been developed by hearing lies and consuming false ideologies has created in us some sort of unjustified fear to take action. This fear becomes even stronger when we see our leaders being killed because they have tried to be different and dare to speak out or to stand for what they believed was good for their nations. When a certain Gadhafi said that Africa was matured, he was killed as a dictator. Perhaps, our leaders were not wise enough to play the mind game. Against hypocrisy, we need to apply hypocrisy and this is what we need.

Those who understand exactly where the battle lies can use appropriate weapon applicable to each situation. But let's remember that the weapons of our warfare are not carnal, but mighty through the pulling down of strong holds. It is not and will never be a physical battle; at least we cannot and should not engage in any physical confrontations. Those of us who have broken the stronghold of self-limitation know exactly that we are more than able.

The way we act and do today is a direct result of the conditioning that fills our subconscious mind. It has been proven scientifically that our unconscious is also where most of our mental habits function.

Whenever we learn to do something with our minds, it becomes automated, and so we become unconsciously skilled at it. Let's take an example of learning to drive a car: at the beginning, it is a conscious act, knowing that we are learning to drive, but after a period of driving regularly, we become used to it and are no longer conscious of what we can do, nor pay close attention to it. At this stage, driving has become natural to us or second nature, we do it as habit and it becomes even pleasurable at this stage because it is easy. It becomes something we will do and do again.

From this example we can see that, depending on whether our actions have negative or positive impact on us, important judgements are made by our own dos and don'ts, i.e. things we should and should not do. Behind our programming, various western companies have developed revenue streams with various items. For example, in recent years we have now rejected our own hair to adopt other people's hair. Real human hair, hair extensions, and this industry make money from over 1.5 billion African people in the four continents. This is a huge market but none of the African countries or people controls this market, even though we are the first consumers.

I will discuss this when we are talking about money bouncing strategies. What is the problem with our hair anyway? We want it to look like others'; we want to be like others, and act like others, denigrating ourselves just because we have not been trained to have confidence in ourselves. We have been trained to respond in this way and we act as expected.

We truly don't know who we are. This is another industry that has been created, and money is made out of African people. Products have been made to lighten our bodies, just as if the bright colour was said to be the best; if we were all light, the world will be boring, we were meant to be different, act differently, each being themself. But through a brain washing exercise, we have been told we are not good enough and, consequently, what we have is not good enough. To be good enough, we need to act and eat what others; wear what they wear and if any part of our body is not like theirs; we can borrow money to buy the experience.

This is either hair, body complexion, or anything else. We sit and wait, they produce it and sell it to us and we happily buy it under the close watch of our children, who will follow our example. What is wrong with this? I say, all is wrong. Let's be ourselves. I am not saying that we should not buy some experiences; I am saying we have all neglected our own values and rubbished what we have to the point that following the trend has become the norm. In the process, we have lost our freedom including the independence our fathers fought hard to get. We know well that they did not plan ahead and that they were conditioned and trained to serve the system that benefited them not, now let's start the transformation process

We can see from Pavlov to Watson that our minds can easily be programmed so that we start believing and doing certain things almost unconsciously. Henceforth, through programming, we can start to accept certain things as normal, without even knowing why. Why do we think that we can't do anything good by ourselves? Why do we think that we need the west to help in everything we do? Why do we think that we are not free? It is because we have been told, and repeatedly told so, to the point that we have no option but to believe this is the case. We have been trained to serve and without question, we serve without knowing that we were serving other people's interests rather than ours.

We were ruled and colonised for over half of a century; most of us were beaten, enslaved, mutilated, many killed, imprisoned, gun power was used and this left the scars in our subconscious to the point that over 50 years afterwards, we continue to transmit this phobia to our children who in turn do the same for their children and so the circle continues.

Our languages were rubbished and a new language taught. It would have been easier to teach us in our own languages, our words would have had more meaning and the system may have reflected our values. We were taught names of places, animals, and things that didn't mean anything to us. These places and things became mystical to us and made us dream of a perfect world which, in our minds, was Europe. Far from it! We were conditioned to think and act in a certain way. To fight and despise our brothers with whom we had lived for thousands of years without any problems.

We were divided and classified by our cultures and facial expressions. Those who were quick to learn to become good servants were called superiors, and this created an atmosphere where none of us wanted to be ourselves any more. We wanted to be like other so-called superiors, who in reality had been the first to be conditioned and alienated. Alienation became the standard and we all wanted unconsciously to become alienated servants without realising it. This stayed in our subconscious and minds. This behaviour continues to be perpetuated. This is what we can still call the colonial subconscious. Yes, years passed and we were becoming aware of our assimilation and domination and started fighting for our independence. Physical independences were obtained but having been well conditioned, we continued to replicate, even in a bad way, what we had been trained for. We were physically free, but consciously and spiritually still colonised. We were still enslaved in our minds and still are probably today.

We are not free if we have no minds of our own. We are

not free if we think our destinies depend on others; yes, others can be useful in our journeys, they may be needed but we need to know where we are going to get help on the way.

What plans did we have for our countries in 50 years' time? What did we want our states to become in 50 years? What did we want our children to become in 100 years' time? We knew we were not free, yet, after taking over, we kept everything that had rendered us captive. We kept the same system. We kept the same type of administration, same education system, same foreign languages, same training for servanthood of our children.

We did not know what was most important to us. We were physically independent but remained servants. Major decisions in our countries were never taken without consulting the master, even up to now, yet we know the masters came to our countries for a purpose. They came to better their lives, to extract resources that they lacked and needed to fuel their growing industries. Africa was their paradise and they certainly made the most of it.

We had no means of producing or exploiting our resources, we asked them to leave because they were enslaving us and using our resources, but we were the ones running after them and begging them to come and use the same resources we initially accused them of stealing, to come back and exploit the same resources.

If their first actions were illegal, we legalised it by inviting them back to our own disadvantage. When we invited them back to exploit our resources, they were free to name the price, we had no choice but to accept; this time, they were not to be held accountable for local development because they were not in charge any more. They were now seen as partners... What partners! Partnership implies a certain degree of respect and equality, yet, we were being told where to sell our resources, what to produce and the prices were imposed upon us.

Because we had been trained as servants, despite thinking that we were free, we were still serving the master. What stupidity. We did not even turn back to study the history and revisit the genesis of our relationship with the ferocious powers. We did not return to understand why they came to us in the first place, even though this was not hidden. They had not changed their objectives; they had not changed the purpose for which they came to our countries in the first instance. They just changed the tactics, because we forced them out. It turned out to be a good thing for them. They can still trade; they can still have their companies, give us jobs so we can serve them. In reality before forging new relationships with them, we should have asked ourselves the following questions:

What was in their minds when they explored the world and what were their intentions when they settled in Africa and Asia? Did they spend their money and time risking their lives to help us and preserve our own interest, or were they trying to fulfil their own ambitions? What type of relationships did they have with us? Have they changed their original intent? Their intention was to stay and exploit as long as possible and they used those they felt at ease to manipulate to consolidate their grip on power and resources. Only those who were good servants were kept close to the central administration. Only those who had learned well were handed over the command.

Just look at the administration everywhere in Africa. Public services are dominated by the ethnic group which has controlled power the most, yet those who truly bring wealth to the country are those with a can-do mentality. Those who own businesses! Businesses pay tax and tax pays public servants. During the colonisation, our people were not trained to build businesses, they were trained to serve and a servant will always be a servant. He will never turn master and will never own anything, except, in fact, if the master confers him this authority.

We all knew that we were being trained to serve. A servant should be docile, not rebellious, and, rather, obedient. A servant should listen and do as he is told. A servant basically has no mind of his own, except in his own house, but at work he is there to serve. A servant is expendable, can be replaced. A servant can be contracted for a limited period. And so our leaders, those who dared to do the contrary, were taught a lesson. Like us all, our leaders were trained to serve and were put in place to serve, by those they served.

This is where it all started. Did we decide on our own educational systems? No, we inherited what we have now. Like I said, a servant may inherit, if the master wills. The master legacy continues today in Africa, just as the master wanted.

Even the Bible recognises that a good servant has the spirit of the master. In Isaiah 42:1–4 it says "Here is my servant, whom I uphold, my chosen one in whom I delight; I will put my Spirit on him." This is true and shows how you recognise a true servant. You want your servant to look after your interests and want to keep those interests as long as they can. We also know that the colonisers or the colonial power was not let by the Spirit of God and were pursuing their selfish interested and used their fellow humans as tools.

They ensured that their servants upheld their values. When they were going, they left those they have trained well to help them further their interest. Since they were not let by the Holy Spirit, the servants inherited their Spirit, their lying spirits instead of the Spirit of truth. So the servants who were left to rule over the nations in Africa upheld their masters' Spirit which was contrary to the Spirit of Good for Africans people. They were serving the colonial powers' interests and not their nations'. That is why in every African nation, they chose those they thought were more loyal and docile to serve.

Those who could not afford to have a mind of their own; and when they tried to have a mind of their own, they were removed. Those to whom the power was given by the colonial power were removed by the colonial powers when they tried to disobey the master. Again, the Bible says the following in Numbers 14:24: "But because my servant Caleb has a different spirit and follows me wholeheartedly, I will bring him into the land he went to, and his descendants will inherit it." You see what is reserved to a good servant? A great reward! That is what most of us were promised and this is how we were divided and this is also how they were persuaded to continue to serve the master, even in a free country.

Our leaders and public servants were all a tool used by the colonial power to serve them. They were conditioned as master/servant relationship all for the purpose of helping the west maintain their domination and overexploitation of African resources.

This song I wrote highlights the irony, the hypocrisy and manipulation we are subject to. It talks about how the west will pretend to be our friend but use and dump us. It talks about their pretence to promote human rights but how wars are maintained when it comes to their interests. It talks about how they laugh with us but bite us behind, how they organise coups against us when we turn our back. This is my song,

it was written when I understood some of the secrets behind our unconscious servanship behavioural patterns.

By the way, in case you don't know yet, my name is Ben, Ben, Mengan, son of Mbii Mengan and Ma'a Mengan. Just listen to my song. As you listen, think about Ben the world changer, the African lover, and the freedom fighter. I will not die by live to see African change, with my stone as a contribution to the building block. My nave will be written in the book of Africans, those who still believe that we can do better. I strongly believe without doubt that we can be better off and that we will surely be, once we move above the colonial subconscious programing.

Just listen to Ben Mengan!

Debout l'Afrique [X2]
Debout l'Afrique oh oh oh
Debout l'Afrique
Stand up Africa! [X3]
I was the first but you made me last
I understand that you stand for right
You kiss my lips and bite my ass
You steal my wealth and use and dump
You lie to my kids and make them fight
I stand alone in a pile of lies
That you brought to light to disguise your intent
What can I do to restore my pride
What can I do to restore my peace?
Debout l'Afrique [X2]
Debout l'Afrique oh oh oh
Debout l'Afrique
Stand up Africa [X3]
Stand up Africa
Stand up Africa and restore your name
I am the one to defend my cause
you need to know I am not a fool

despite your arms our kids will fight
Stand up Africa and defend your name

Yes, we need to stand up and defend our name, we need to stand up and clear the mess. We need to reach out within to destroy the bomb that was planted in our mind, which has disabled our ability to see ourselves as we truly are. Men and women of valour, let's stand up. We are capable, and able to do anything. Nothing is impossible to all human beings. Impossibility is a self-imposed limitation. Are we not of the same species as them? We need to move from servanthood to take our place in the leadership of the world. We claimed our land and got it back, we need to act now as rightful owners and proprietors. We need to be proud people. Proud people don't beg, they don't depend on anyone else. They rely on their strengths and they know their worth. Proud people don't sell themselves cheap. They are simply confident in themselves and their abilities. Are we? Let's show it.

This starts with our refusal to accept stereotypes. We are not black, we are Africans. We are not sad and hungry, this doesn't qualify us, we are just in the process of discovering how to use our land and resources better. Our present conditions are but a temporary events and it has happened because we have slept a bit. Now that we are awake, things will change. We are taking charge; we are standing up, Africa! We are standing up to take our place.

We reject all negative qualifications and classifications that put us down. We reject anything that portrays us in a negative way. We are Africans, those who gave birth to the first civilization. The continent where all human beings came from!

When I was growing up, I was told there were four races, white, red, yellow and back. Today, we only hear about white and black even though I have never seen a truly black person; we have let this go on and accept that we are black, with no objections. Others have refused this labelling and, as result, no one dares to label them. We are unique, we are Africans, when we talk about Africa, it is us in the south of Sahara. Others say that they are Arabs. So no more black. We can do with African labelling but we reject back labelling. We are a blessed generation and we have been given the privilege to know the truth. We will ensure that this truth is brought to light so that we can all be free. Only the truth can liberate and here we are seeking and exposing the truth to conquer our true freedom. We want to go from servants to owners, from helpers to makers, from beggars to givers. In fact we are givers whose low self-esteem has turned into beggars. We are reclaiming our place, standing taller amongst the giants. We make our way as equal partners and reclaim the respect we deserve through self-affirmation. We are no longer servants; we are going from savant to masters, from bound to freed, from down to up, from silent to speakers, from beggars to givers, from users to inventors. We are people of valour who have helped every continent. Our children built the most powerful economy of the earth, we are claiming our share. Let see how the servant gets his freedom.

Chapter 5:

The servant's freedom

Our common tragedy is not that we are poor, but it is our poverty mind-set. In order words, we are not poor but we simply believe that we are poor despite our incomparable wealth. If we were poor, I wouldn't be writing this book. Thankfully we are not. The greatest mistake of African people is not our lack of wealth; - we are extremely rich; but the irony is that we don't acknowledge what we have. We are rich within, and our land is a paradise sough after. But funnily we behave like strangers in our own land. Even when we become aware of the extent of what we have, we don't appreciate it, as a result, and we don't find out how to value it.

When I talk about the colonial subconscious we need to be clear that I am otherwise stressing the fact that we can transcend what we have been fed with unconsciously from the moment we start to have a deeper understanding of a blank cheque we have been given at birth. Right from the beginning of mind kind, a mandate to subdue, multiply and replenish the earth was given all human beings no matter what race or continent they came from. So African like any other human species is able to subdue, multiply and replenish the earth. All Africans have this potential that we can turn into wealth. This is our blank cheque, yet we, African people, have refused to write it to ourselves. We wait for other to write it to us and by so doing, we remain in bondage, acting like servants, living in complete poverty.

We have fallen into a trap of believing what we are told we are, rather than finding out what and who we truly are from within. The example of Gideon in the Bible shows how a simple understanding of our potential can chance our story and history. How a simple encouragement and enlightenment or how a reminder of our true worth can transform our mind-set.

In Judges 6:11-13, we see that the angel of the LORD came and sat under the oak that was in Ophrah, which belonged to Joash the Abiezrite as his son Gideon was beating out wheat in the wine press in order to save it from the Midianites. So we understand here that Gideon was afraid, wanted to hide his wheat before the Midianites took it by force.

The angel of the LORD appeared to him (Gideon) and said to him, "The LORD is with you, O valiant warrior." When he was called a mighty man of valour, Gideon was perplex but this somehow gave him the courage to believe that he was worthy. We can see that after he was called a mighty man of valour, Gideon has the courage to ask for signs to prove that what was said of him was true. When the Angel of the lord confirmed that he was truly a great person, when he was told that within himself, he had the ability to become a leader, he changed and further down in the Bible, Judges Chapter 6, Gideon went on to win the battle and became the leader of Israel.

He did not go through any special training, just a simple recognition of who he was, of his true potential was enough to lift him above the crown of cowards people and turned him into a president of a nation as he lead the

Israelite into battle and victory. Just by recognising that he was strong and of value was enough for him to use the power and potential that was already in him. This came as an announcement to him by someone, but he believed that he was what the person said he was.

So, I am saying that African people are able people and I hope that this will wake the genius sleeping in African people. We have evidence from the Bible that a simple motivating word transformed Gideon's experience and his mental determination helped him to become a self-proclaimed leader who led his people to victory. He went from a shied fearful man to a feared leader, from an under achiever to a history maker. In every one of us, there is a Gideon, we are leaders, winners, achievers, transformers, inventers and we are all valuable to Africa.

Pastor Tudor Bismarck once said that "there is a reason why we are born where we are born and that there is a reason why we come from one particular family". "We shouldn't worry about what is happening now; our situation now will always make it look like nothing is possible", Pastor Matthew Ashimolowo always says. We are free, but only in our mind can we be free. We should have not only one year plan but 50 years plan". I do agree with Pastor Tudor Bismarck that If we had planned from the independence, we should have been free by now, but we were busy trying to control power and whatever small resources were left when the colonial power departed without even understanding what we were getting ourselves into. We were busy thinking about ourselves and we continue to want only for ourselves. Our leaders have done it, passed it on to their children, whom have grown up with the wrong mentality and ideals.

If we as future leaders of our nations had brought up our children to think country, think future, they would not have deviated. But our past leaders and present continue in the same vein as their predecessors if not worse and we all see the results today. Africa and African people's conditions have worsened. One person can deviate but not all. So if all African people are doing badly, it is the evidence that there is structurally and fundamentally something wrong that needs addressing.

Few citizens can deviate but not a whole generation like it is the case now and before our time. If the whole generation is thinking selfishly, if the whole generation is willing to sell their country cheap, there must be something wrong in the way the past generation has made, raise us up and trained us to think.

The worst is that we think that the solution for our problem can come from somewhere else. We all count on funding, projects financed by people from outside the continent. We wait for others to find a solution for us. That is our mental illusion. If we are constantly counting and waiting on others to solve our problems, this means in reality that we depend on those people. If we count on the west to transfer their technologies that they spend time and money to discover, if we wait for the west to discover the cure for HIV, if we wait for the west to come out with the cure for malaria, we are in fact saying that we depend on them for our lives, our futures, our sick, our welfare, our resources, our people.

In fact we are saying that we depend on them for our survival. Let's be clear, they don't come out with new technologies for free, they spend money and time to come out with these inventions and they do it because they want to make money, more money from their discoveries. Their aim is to make money as long as they can from a single discovery, so if they have their way, they will maintain us under contract as long as they can so they can make as much as they are able to.

Those who make money selling medication can create diseases if they find a cure before - this is morally wrong but I will not discard this option- So they can make money from it. Those who make money selling cars want to sell their cars and as well as car parts as long as possible. Those who make money selling ideologies will maintain their ideologies as long as they can, so they can remain in business. So, if they can get money maintaining malaria, they will maintain it as long as they can.

They don't want to go out of business. We understand that malaria is our problem, not anyone else's, because we suffer from it and we can find solutions in Africa.

We can't become free without acknowledging our current status and reviewing what constitutes a handicap to our freedom. Free people are those who count on themselves and do not depend on others. They can collaborate with others giving and taking but when you are a consumer, not a producer, you can only take what is given to you. If you don't want it, you better produce what you need. If however, you chose to always take what is given to you, you will become dependent and at the mercy of the giver; unfortunately Africans are at this stage.

So can we say that African is free? If not, why and what is the cause of this lack of freedom? When Africa gets help from somewhere, the help comes necessarily from those trying to help themselves, consequently, we become worse by receiving help and support which only comes with a price tag.

In fact, in our struggle to get assistance, we end up serving others and their causes rather that solving our original problems. We go out with one problem to solve and come back with two others: debt servicing and over dependence. Instead of crying for the transfer of technologies, let's focus on creating a vibrant technologic movement in our continent. Let's get our children working and researching for what we need. Let's start the process of building the machines that we need. Those machines are built by human beings like us. Let's build cars, let's find cures for diseases, let's teach our children the process of doing things by themselves. One step at a time with a belief that we will get there! Let's focus our energies in the sectors that we see as important until we get the result we want. We just need the will power.

Physically we are free but mentally, spiritually or psychologically we also need to be free, therefore, our fight becomes a spiritual fight, not a physical fight. This fight needs to start with our own minds before we can proceed to other people's minds. We need strategies to overcome our current limiting factors. Physically we will never win.

We have no sophisticated weapons, no access to sophisticated arsenals and we have even signed an agreement never to pursue or undertake to make atomic weapons. We signed for the International Criminal Court of Justice, which has become a central stage to judge and condemn us. Our presidents are the only ones who are judged at The Hague. If Gaddafi had not been assassinated, he would have been brought there to be judged; he was killed along with members of his family and the country lost thousands of people; this has not been reported as a crime against humanity and the perpetrators are still giving lessons to the world. While Iraq is still going pear shaped, no one had been brought to justice in Europe for causing such an atrocity. We understand that Saddam killed thousands of people; not that we accept what he did, but we say that there was a way to resolve the issue, not to add more damage to what had already been done.

We have to remember that no one is eternal and

sometimes, by letting people go naturally; we can avoid catastrophes and impose an orderly transition without bloodshed. As we all know by now, no one is safe in Iraq more than 10 years after Saddam was killed, but who takes responsibility? Those who committed this crime have never and will never be brought to account. People may carry out inquiries and conclude that the war was wrong and immoral, but was it a crime against humanity? I don't know the definition of as a crime against humanity, I leave this to experts. I am just looking at how the balance of power works. In this context, can we really risk any physical confrontations? No, the result is predicted long before the beginning. But we can win, if we tap into the unseen world of our imagination and creative will, where everything is conceived before manifestation. This needs to start in our own minds, we need to believe that we are truly able and free to undertake anything that can benefit the human species as a whole and we need to believe that we and can do what we want, without risking any physical fight with anyone.

Once we have the real solutions, we can engage in what people will call diplomacy, tactics, ideological positioning to defend our interest. After all, there are no relationships amongst nations other than that of interests. Knowing that we are still servants, my next question is how can we truly come out of our servant hood position? This is the question of how a servant can become free.

Simplistically, the servant can be adopted into the master's family, in real life, the master may grant freedom to the servant or the forces for change can become so strong that the master has no choice but to surrender. This has happened in the past. The masters did not just give up. They were forced to give up and this was not through a war, it was through diplomacy, the outcry of people, the condemnation etc. In South Africa, apartheid was not wilfully abandoned by the minority who held power and privileges. It was made possible as a result of rallies and international efforts as well as persistence of the victims.

The last option for freedom is the rebellion of the servants and this carries serious consequences for the servant because the master may treat them worse. This is what Africa has been going through. We acquired our independence by force and have paid the price for over 50 years.

But today in the 21st century, nations are more mature than before and the world is becoming richer, opportunities are greater than before and giving up certain privileges will not necessarily render rich nations poorer. With people more informed than ever before, with humanists abounding in every corner of the earth, our hope is a wave of revolution, which if simultaneously engaged in every corner of the continent, will bring positive change. This is possible and forces for change are forever at work, better than before.

The whole continent is tired and people are ready. Heads of states themselves are fed up; though for now they can only wait and pray that the people start the movement, even though they fear it may cost them their position. This scenario can be avoided if those playing the masters understand our true nature as human beings and respect, as they proclaim and sing loud that the respect human rights. Our true nature as human beings or our brotherhood with Christ Jesus is the best way out. This should be a simple scenario when our fellow world citizens consciously accept that enough is enough and that we all deserve a better treatment.

This happened in the Bible where Onesimus became free when Philemon understood that he was an equal human being like him, through Christ Jesus. Paul's diplomatic strategies played a pivotal role in Onesimus' freedom. Similarly, a diplomatic negotiation will be core to our true liberation, but this should be done simultaneously with a core and structural mental reprogramming of our mind-set- through a well prepared education system within the continent. I mean that diplomatic negotiations should be sustained by a strong will for our mental freedom when we start adopting programmes that reflects our needs. When in schools, universities and our public sectors we have changed the way we do things, when our children are raised with a sense of responsibility and self-confidence, when we reject aid and over dependency, we will be ready and can go to brothers in other nations to negotiate freely. When we are ready, it will be evident and brothers will rise up from all corners of the earth, like Paul did for Onesimus, convincing Philemon, to set him free. Similarly, people of mental abilities will join us in our fight and the most stubborn of our time should realise that it is time to let go. This can happen in no time at all, this does not require another 50 years. It can happen in two to five years if we are ready. Our readiness can happen like in the case on Gideon with a sudden regain of consciousness of our true worth and an act of self-confidence put into practice.

In Philemon, we see that Paul convinced Philemon to do the right thing. Paul did not want to order him to do it. We need to have advocates that will convince the most stubborn that losing the grip on Africa was the right thing to do. But our behaviour will determine how people advocate for us. For example if we put an end to our own corrupt and self-serving habits. I will put this strongly later using facts and examples.

We see that Onesimus ran away from his master, but

came to Paul an apostle, the guardian of faith, an example of good character and moral at the time, the one who wants gave examples and guide the world on issues of right or wrong; nowadays we can point to some nations that take the leadership in this area and ask them to be courageous enough to admit their won wrong and torts and become our advocates, our defenders. These nations or countries can be like Paul or at least play Paul by convincing or requesting former colonial powers to let go. Perhaps if we change our strategies, like Onesimus did with Paul, if we start to behave well, but most of all, this will trigger this types of actions. But if we don't those people can also be wise enough to act like Paul, who had already understood our equality in God's eyes, knew and adopted Onesimus as a brother, even though he was superior to him. He even wanted to keep Onesimus with him, but asked Philemon to agree to this.

In the book of Philemon, we see a true moral value, not the talking, and this world police can do the same. The USA and the United Kingdom, if they take the lead in resolving this issue, the grip on Africa and interference by other nations will be loosened. This can be done in no time, provided we are ready and start the diplomatic ball rolling.

Knowing God's values and the right thing to do, Philemon, I am sure, freed Onesimus. We all know issues around human rights and the sovereignty of states and their right to decide on their own affairs. It will be the right thing to for those who hold Africa captive with all sorts of strategies to lose their grip. It will be the right thing to condemn those who try to cause trouble in countries because of calculated gains. Parallel to our situation, I may ask who guarantees our freedom. Who wants to set the standard in the world? Who wants to combat bad governance and corruption? Who wants a free world where human rights are respected and human values are recognised? Does this person or country exist? I would say yes. I call upon your authority that, in light of the high moral values you hold you should have a head to head conversation with your allies and decide to set the servant free. Bring down barriers, blocks and bilateral relations that do nothing else than serve your only interests whilst keeping Africa underneath.

This freedom will now encompass every area of our life, starting with challenging stereotypes that make people believe no good things can come from Africa, and, following on, dismantling the systems that have been put in place to hold us back. As we work on our own minds, please use your influence to make this happen. Never mind what Africa has got and what is being used, we can all share and still help each other, for years. There is a new way we can do this, without killing people and without pointing fingers. The issue is in the open, the west wants to maintain the leadership position and they want these resources. There is a way to negotiate new deals, based on fairness, and share gains with the principles of freedom as a central point for our endeavours.

Internally we have a new pledge; to run our administration the way we should, our teachers, our police force, our ministers, our governors will all abide by the code of professional practice as responsible citizens. They will have a job description, where presently there is none. Since our present education system contributes to making us servants, we will change it to meet our needs. Our children will know that we are waiting for them to come up with solutions to cure diseases, to build heavy machineries, to come up with new technologies. Our researchers will know the burden that they carry, to free us from over dependence on foreign imports. Our farmers will know that we are waiting for their produce to feed our people. Our bankers will know that our economic system depends on the way they understand our culture and reform the banking system to respond to our needs. Money needs to be replenished to serve the nation whilst making more money. Money needs to produce money, value needs to be added to everything we do and in every sector when we have understood our people and work with them.

We will no longer focus on the wrong things, just because we want to be like others. Look at Europe. Holland is not like Germany and Italy is not like Spain or France even though they are neighbours. They copy good this from other nations whilst remaining themselves and keeping their values which marks their differences, despite having their own national vision and priorities. We need to look forward and walk forward. We need to set our aims high and go for the sky. This means that we need to abandon the crab walk. Therefore to avoid this crab walk, let see how we have been walking till now. When we walk backward whilst looking forward, we are doing the crab walk.

Chapter 6:
Empty hopes and crabs walk

Crabs walk backwards; likewise Africa appears to move; we look forward but our actions, deeds and movements are pulling us backward. The state of our roads, our corrupt and chaotic administrative systems, our way to live in the past and hold the missing to account is what makes our daily living. We don't plan ahead if not for the next election, this is for those in politics, and as soon as we get into office, we think only about ourselves as we alone deserve the best, so, as long as we are profiting from our position, the rest can go to hell. We think not for the future generations, and 50 years appears to be far beyond what we believe we can live long enough to see. Therefore the future is not worth the waste of our time. So, as we act in this manner on a day by day, we revert back to where we were when they came to steal our kids to build the wealth they enjoy today.

For ordinary people, we plan on a daily basis, counting on luck and handouts, God willing! When we greet people, we expect them to respond with hands in their pockets, and when we see those who are better off, we are sure we have hit the jackpot as in our minds, we think they can change our lives. We are always dreaming and counting on fairy tales, hoping that one day, somehow we will wake up wealthier than ever, out of the blue.

So we expect our miracles every day but we forget that miracles happen where human beings are unable to reach. Miracles will not happen for things we can do by ourselves. If we want to improve our living conditions, we have to work for it, and this starts by using the brain we were given for free to use at will. We are not intelligent by mistake; we are so made so we can make use of it. No one else can change our lives but ourselves.

What do we see? We see that day by day, our wish is to gain the most for ourselves and our households, when we are placed somewhere to work, amassing as much as we can, so the rest can go to our natural children. If we are clever enough, not to waste it all in pubs and bars for the pleasure that brings nothing new to the feast. Yet the rest can die beside and around our mansions, we care less if we have nothing to gain. Without the roads we still can reach our retreat home in faraway villages by helicopters. The mess along the way, we know it not, because we can afford to fly above without the pain of driving in dirty forests. For what is the need for us to care, when we can enjoy the wealth of all when it's our time? Because others are doing the same, and more will join the queue to do the same, when our time to grab the state resources -what I call the national self-help moment has come to an end-. We can't afford to lose the gain; for this we were put in place to serve ourselves with the goods of all.

We make our fortune and that's the way it goes in this part of the world, and if we live long enough to reach the time afar, we can only regret the fact that those who have come behind us have taken our place to do worse than we did in our time.

When we retire and stand aside, we become the judges and see ourselves as saints because what we did, in our mind, was less than what our replacement are doing now.

Despite the good lessons we left behind- we know for sure we are not good example to follow-, we think as if we were not responsible for what others are doing now, yet they learned from us, what now applies as rules to run our public offices. As we become the judges and see ourselves as saints, since our mind is telling us that what we did was less than what they are doing now, we give the lessons we did not apply when we had the chance to change the country. We can't stop a moment to think and see that those we left to serve are following our path as good students. Despite the lessons we left behind, we think as if we were not responsible for what now applies as rules- embezzling at will. We think they should stop. We even attempt to confront them but they openly remind us about what we did. Ashamed and confused, we resign and shut our mouth.

We see the west as the model to copy in every area of our lives going forward but when it comes to our corrupt behaviour, we think that a good professional code of conduct is solely reserved for them and we start to blame them for all our vices, despite our self-serving habit being the cause of the decay of what was left behind, which is now all gone, as we ignore that we are partly to blame for our demise.

Despite the fact that they were serving themselves when they were in our land, they nonetheless built the roads to carry the loads away, and by so doing we also used to walk on them and used them for our journeys to farms or cities. But because we – the new masters – live around and can fly home, there is no point wasting what rightfully belongs in our pockets in the interest of all the rest. Therefore no new roads built. We will use the state money to buy helicopters and use them to fly home where necessary.

Who we know can pinch a bit and with luck, they can

earn a seat in the corner that can profit their own family members, provided that we have a piece of what they take from it all. Our joy will be full to the brim that they have learned to gain and amass like us and, whilst remembering us, those who gave them the chance to earn the right to steal. So the years will pass and less and less will the masses earn from what we said belongs to all.

The roads we saw on the way to Mengan remind us how far back we have gone, but what to care for, when we have all we need to live today and can leave the crumbs to our own family, as long as they have access and a glimpse of hope in what we have now for their future? There is no need to worry about what others may say, for this is our way of life and naught will change as long as we stand to earn from our mess. The mess becomes the norm because it is good for now and for us. The mess and chaos we create serves the interest of the business we are in. Our place here for sure is not for long; so why the wait to start enjoying from the pot from which we lose nothing for emptying or breaking? If after us the deluge arrives, the loss belongs to those behind. The bridge on which we stand can serve the purpose now, at once, as long as we cross to board; that is what matters the most and the rest can drown and perish. It is not our problem!

If you talk about conscience, we point to others because they are the cause of what we have become. Yes, this is not for us to change because we will be the one at loss, and to care is, for sure, proof of our foolishness; but to show that we are not foolish, we act like we do to prove to all that we are sage.

One points to those who teach our children for as long as 50 years to end up poor or those who can see with their eyes and refuse to join the queue, and do like the rest have done. As for us, we see their act as the ways of mad people, for fools alone can act alike as, for sure, it is clear that the impact of our actions is less on self. We are losing nothing; only the public is paying the price.

The country bears the costs and pays the price; that is it! Yet those who have managed to resist are proud to say that they alone have not been like the rest, and that for sure they will give account for what they did to destroy the wealth of the nation they were supposed to preserve when they were put in charge to serve.

What was the point of chasing the colonial powers out if we are set to do worse than them? The hope we sold to all our own to entice our young to join the fight was nothing but empty promises. They understood it when they were sent back empty handed, like Mbii, my Dad; when they raised their fist, they were told to shut it, when the time was come to enjoy as promised.

My Dad was free from the army with nothing to his name after all the years he served the land, and it is not to say there wasn't enough to give him a penny for the days ahead. It is not because we are here in the south that we lack the opportunities. All we need is our state of mind. To prove I am right, we take the people from the south-Africa and put them in the west, and take people from the west and bring them to Africa. We leave the state of the each place the way they are for now, the west with its wealth and built assets intact for Africans to enjoy when we get there, and Africa's land with the mess left for the west to struggle with it like we are struggling now when they arrive.

Each group is moved to a new land and I am sure the first years we will spend in the west will be the best as we use what was left behind. Because we were programmed as servants, users and losers, we will act the same when we get to the west and will use without planning what they have left, changing nothing, in the same way we did when the colonial power left Africa after the independences – with this mentality, we ended up getting lost in our own land. Today we see the west as the best, but I am sure those who built it had no more hands or eyes than us – or had they two heads, unlike us?

The swap is still taking place and now each group will spend 20 years in their new land. Let's be clear, we give each group 20 years to enjoy or struggle with the place in which they have been placed; at the end the 20 years, we check the state of the places. The south would have transform like the west and the west would reversed to the mess in the same way the south was before the swap, because African people with their present mentality would have taken their way of life to the west. Their programming to be small-mind people at the beginning and during and after the colonial period would have obliged them to use all without replenishing, despite the order they met and the wealth they enjoyed at first when they were transferred to the west. At the end of the 20 years swap, they would have eaten and used without reserves or plans, just like it is the case do now, and at the end, they would have emptied all and imposed their present mess amidst.

With this example, we see now that the wealth was not in the place, but far from there; it was in the minds. The west transferred to the south would have struggled at first but won the fight through careful planning, research, investigative power and constant investment in their future in the land we saw as mess. Looking at this, it becomes clear that the state of our land is down to us and how we plan to get the best from should be our duty.

For this, it is hard to claim the theft because we became the ones we accused of being the cause of our misfortunes. As long as we keep our minds the way they are now, it will be hard to move ahead. The system has something to do with it but we are free to change at will the way we train our kids to act, and the way we choose to live our lives, because the country starts from the family cell; and one by one, we add to the rest, and all of us, we become the people of the land. So let's start the change we want to see in the child to whom we gave life, and in whom we pour our minds, as the advice and training we give at home will help him to make his way in life.

So, the change in the land should start at home. As long as we do the right thing, we should care less for what others are doing, and as long as most impart the best to those who are growing up now; we are sure our fight for right will live and stand long after we have crossed to the other side. But even from there we can hold our heads higher and give account for what we did for ourselves and the land in which we were put to change and to give the best we had.

Now if we have done as we were meant to do, there is hope to live beyond the now for me and all who are mine. It wasn't supposed to be like this when we engaged in the fight to free ourselves. The least we hoped for was to have enough to eat every day; we wanted to have in abundance and forever; but now the hope has turned to despair, and poverty becomes the enemy to fight. Yet the land contains the best and it is still virgin, ready to give the best of all we wish for all our needs.

Here and there, old and young cry alike for food, as they are consumed by poverty. Perhaps it's time to paint the picture of what this vice looks like, so all may taste from afar if they have never seen such or been in such a state in their lives. For me I came from there, and it is hard to forget, despite the wealth I bathe in now. This is the call for all of us, to act together so lives can change forever. We went from abundance to lack, from plenty to poverty when we started to follow the way of life of others. We thought the western way was the best and we left all in pursuit of what we ignored was able to reduce us to beggars and servants. We left our way of life in search of a better way of life, which ended up in poverty. Now our people have a fight on their hands. Poverty! This is why I say that we walk like crab. Even though I was not around, I am not sure we were not so hungry before our independences. Perhaps we have always been poor, but our past cannot justify why we are still at this stage of impoverishment at this particular point of the world's development.

Poverty is not going empty for a single day and getting something to eat the next day; instead, poverty is going empty with no hope for the future. Poverty is getting nobody to feel your pain, and poverty is when your dreams go in vain because nobody is there to help you. Poverty is watching your mothers; fathers, brothers and sisters die in pain and in sorrow just because they couldn't get something to eat. Poverty is hearing your grandmothers and grandfathers cry out for death to come and take them because they are tired for the future. Poverty is getting nobody to feel your pain, grandchildren die in your arms; but there is nothing you can do. Poverty is watching your children and grandchildren shed tears in their deepest sleep.

Poverty is suffering and dying a shameful death, with nobody seeming to care; hopelessly waving goodbye when you are dying or seeing them die without medication or support. Poverty is when you hide your face and wish nobody could see you just because you feel less than a human being. Poverty is when you dream of bread and fish you have never seen in the daylight. Poverty is when people accuse you and persecutes you for no fault of yours;

but who is there to say something for you? Poverty is when the hopes of your fathers and grandfathers just vanish and vanish with the blink of an eye. I know poverty, and I know poverty just like I know my father's name. Poverty never sleeps. Poverty works all day and night in Africa, helped by war and diseases, but when its leaders either pretend nothing is happening or beg to feed themselves, this attitude gives poverty no holidays.

An African president sees no poverty but this is the day to day life for 80% of our people. Yet over 60 years ago, it wasn't so bad and that is why I say we have copied the crabs, looking ahead and walking backwards without seeing where we are going. For this is not different from having blindness for life. What is the point of pretending to walk when we know not where we are heading to? What is the point of saying we know, when we ignore all of what should be done? Jesus said that if we were blind, this was excusable, but because we are blind and pretend to see, this is what hurt him the most. Because he could see that we were lost and proud still to say we knew. Instead of holding our hands up, we are proud and refuse to recognise our doom.

As most people continue to live in extreme poverty despite all we have, it is only fair and right for us to stop for a few seconds or for a minute to think about what has made other nations richer and how together we can win the war against hunger and lack. Instead, we continue to beg for food as if we were animals unable to fend for ourselves. I condemn the aid and we are going stop it. Yes, we need to discuss aid; what I call spoon-feeding aid.

If our people have more to do to earn better, they will rely less on handouts. If we create manufactures and services that will increase our people's earning potentials,we wouldn't need to give them handouts. In fact, handouts keep them bound and down. Every day our people die because of poverty yet, there are countless numbers of organisations fighting against poverty in Africa! Millions of people cannot access medical treatment because of poverty. Our doctors cannot do much to save lives because of lack and penury and this has hardened their heart and tarnishes their profession. All this is due to the same poverty we have been fighting for 50 years through various aid programmes.

Some examples, to name but a few: I went to the hospital as soon as I arrived, I saw on the floor a man covered in blood. He had been the victim of a road accident; a Samaritan had managed to bring him to the hospital, as the family was not aware, no one dared to care, because to receive their care, he needed to pay. Perhaps he even had money in his pockets, but unable to move or talk he could not advocate his case; yet doctors and nurses passed by, ignoring the sufferings of a citizen for whom there was a need to care. I asked if they knew the clock was ticking for this man to cross to eternity. They said they knew that, although an intervention could hold back fate and give the man another chance to live, they couldn't move a foot without the francs. Yes, without a deposit, there was no way they could act despite the suffering and agony he was in. I begged and begged but no one seemed to care, so, the only way to save this life was to put my hand in my pocket. As soon as I did, they rushed him in for treatment and, bit by bit, he imposed respect when they found out later who his relatives were. But without my help, he would have died in front of doctors for whom money was the prime, the only way to make them care.

I was told this is the rule for all to follow in all our public hospitals. I remember the days before my move abroad, just years after the west had left, and all were still able to receive free care at first before they were given a list of medicine to add on top of those they had for free. Yes our population has grown but if with what we have, we were able to plan ahead, our people would still be able to receive some form of care for free.

For this I thought of a crab, which walks backwards with its face frontward. As if this alone was not enough, I saw a woman rushed in from a prison who was in labour full of pain. It was established straight away that she needed a caesarean but £10 was needed to rent equipment and for medication; the doctors and nurses refused to do anything unless the required money was paid in advance. I begged again but all was in vain. As I had already emptied my pockets to save the first victim, I promised to bring the sum and asked for the treatment to start while I rushed to the bank to draw the cash. But this was falling on deaf ears, and soon they left the woman to fight for her life. I took the cab to the nearest cashpoint and on my return, the woman had passed away with the child in her womb, and the body was pushed aside awaiting someone who could claim the remains to bury.

I was called aside by a wise nurse who advised me that I would soon be exhausted because cases like this are thousands a day, and they had become immune to the suffering because this was the norm in our land. It was a system they didn't like but with all their will, nurses and doctors could not reverse it because resources were lacking and the only way to help the sick was for them to bear the costs.

Again and again, I thought of a crab, and knew our country had become like one. After this day of pain, I returned home, but to forget the day I decided to drive around to cool my nerves; but as I drove I saw the police in my mirror asking me to stop. As I stopped they asked for paperwork, and no matter which paper was given, they couldn't care less, for they were after me for one thing alone. The bribe they are used to collecting, as they serve themselves like all the others who hold positions in the country public office. What a day; but this was less compared with other days because I did not have to sign anything; if I had, it would have been worse.

This is the way our country has worked since the days we chased the west away.

Let's have a last look of what is wrong with ourselves as we move forward for better. When I look everywhere in Africa, I can see the same corruption, the same mentality, the same laziness, the same lack of respect for public property, the same embezzlement of public funds, the same lateness to work and so on. In reality, we do nothing to deserve the respect. If we don't deserve the respect of our own citizens, how do we want others to respect us?

I said I wanted to check by myself, and went to a police station with a friend who has no Identity card. I said to a police officer whom I approach, this person has no ID, he is my friend and I need your help. The police officer ushers us in; in bright day light he said, "I can help you but it will cost you. To do your ID you need a citizenship certificate, your birth certificate, if you don't have it, I can do it for you now and here." There and then he collects £10 and in five minutes he has written things and signs them himself and in 10 minutes all was done. He collected the money and pocketed it. I looked around; there was an old lady with all the documents required, genuine and correct, she had been coming and going back for a week, but because she has no money to give for free, no one seems to care.

I said I will wait and see what will happen to this senior citizen. This ID was not needed; it was just my way to verify the facts. My friend invited the police officer for lunch after he had finished his identity card. This police officer left the office immediately and followed us. It was not lunch time yet and my friend did not expect him to come right then. In his own words, the police officer says, "Let's go now, you have made my day!" Still a long queue of citizens waited for service; those who had paid were moved from the back of the queue to the front and served. Those with nothing never received the service.

Here we went to the bar where, at this time of the day, my newly found friend was supposed to be at work. We talked. The policeman asked me, "Where do you live?" I said, "In Europe." And then he said, "You should have paid more for the service I rendered to you. We have two prices, a price for those who live here, and a price for those who come from abroad. Because you have more money, you should pay more. It is only in small services like yours that we can realise something for our families. Our salaries are peanuts and side money like this gives us the means to live decently. You don't understand us, we are here; working hard and receiving peanuts as salaries and this is how we manage to survive." Then we start to talk about the situation in the country.

He accuses the president of getting the biggest salary and being corrupt and living in luxury whilst they, worthy citizens, were suffering. He talked about ministers, how they travelled abroad all the time and as soon as they are appointed they build mansions from the money they get from contracts they have signed with foreign countries that should have been paid into the government treasury. Then we talked about other services. My man told me how he, as a police officer, will pay a bribe in order to be allowed to pay for his water bill. He said, "You see? People are corrupt in this country, we police officers are here to put order in the country but when I see an officer taking the bribe for me to pay the tax or my bills, I try to warn them, but they don't even care."

My man discussed with us how foreigners are better treated than nationals; for example, they come with their money and get the service as quickly as they want. As an example, he told me how he wanted to register his land. This process took him four years, but someone with money came and did it in two months. He talked about how our woods, our timbers, our petrol, our gas, our diamonds, our gold, and all our resources were being thrown away for free. We talked and talked as he drank and drank until he became drunk at this time of the day when he was supposed to be serving the country. No, he was not in the office at all, and did not care that he was using his working time for leisure. This concept did not exist in his language. He was entitled to do this, including ripping citizens off for services that they should have had for free. He was telling me he loved his country so much and was doing his best and will stand firm against corruption. He added finally that all these corrupt politicians and ministers should be put in jail. He pointed out a country that has done so and corrupt ministers were being put in jail for their actions. "In Cameroon," he said, "the president is putting all these culprits in prison." I look at him and asked, "Do you think it is a good thing to put all the corrupt people of this land in jail?" Without thinking and with enthusiasm and a sign of relief to show his prayers have been answered he said at once, "Yes! Yes, of course, of course! That is what we all want in this country. If you ask any citizen, he will be in agreement. This is the only way this country will go forth. Normally those people selling our country for cheap, those people squandering our resources and those people ripping off our citizens should be put in jail." He added again, "If I was a president, I would make sure corruption is banned". "As a police officer," he told me, "we have laws in this country but people don't follow them."

I looked and looked at him, as he appeared not to know the reasons for my looks. In fact, he was sure he was righteous because the culprits were others, not him. After all, what has he done that was worthy of judgement? I looked and looked at him and asked at last, "What do you think about the police force?" He said, "We are doing our job the best we can. The only thing is that the government don't give us what we deserve. We work very hard. You saw the queue waiting to be served. This is how it goes every day." I asked again, "Do you want to go back now and serve, as you say there is a long queue?" "Oh no," he said, "I need to take my time; we are talking about something important here. I don't care if they spend all their days there! After all, it is not every day that I have these opportunities to dine with wealthy people like you." I asked that he should be given more to eat and drink. At this point, I was already unable to contain my anger and I said, "I saw you collecting the money from the public, from the citizens you say you love. You collected money from my friend; do you think you should be put in jail as well? What do you think you are doing? Isn't it a corruption you are complaining against? Don't you think you should be in jail too for corruption?" He changed the tone of his voice. "You know, my friends, this is not the country of white people. This is Africa and this is the way it goes here. Don't try to bring that your nonsense here, here is here, there is there. This is our reality, everyone does this and this is how the system works. I don't do like ministers or other people high up there. They get more money than me. Even a small clerk collects money, this is how they manage to build a house or send their children to school. Our salaries are not enough."

I asked again, "Do you think this is similar to what you want to see condemned?" He hesitated and said it was not. He was just getting tips from his job, he said. Our man, who was condemning the country, condemned himself but refused to admit he was one of those who were bringing the country down to its knees. What do you think? It is up to us all now to judge. We need to be the change we want to see in others. Yes, the change must start with us.

We point the finger to others as if we are not at fault. You see my friend; the cause of our problems is never down to anyone else but us. We are all responsible for our demise. Each of us bears responsibility for our common future. Each of us has a role to play and each of us has to engage in the fight against, corruption, embezzlement, lack of responsibility, professional misconduct and injustice. The fight is in our own hands. But yet each of us shifts the blame to others. You see, even as corrupt as he was, our police officer didn't even realise the extent of his action because the practice has become a norm and daily routine.

As long as we shift the blame away, nothing will ever change. Are we free or not? Was my friend free to serve or not? Each change we want to see happen should start with us right now. This is what I call true freedom. Our faith in ourselves and our ability to manage our salaries, our ability to find a more creative way to complement our salaries will be a key for our personal financial freedom. Some can have a small business on the side, some can become inventors, business people, and this is not forbidden, provided there is no conflict of interest with our profession because this will alter our judgement.

In contracts, the giving away of our resources is done

by people like us. We think that if we were there, the case would be different; not at all if we do not change within before we start. Nothing will change until each of us starts to change and this change should start within, at home, at work to the point that it becomes our way of life. Freedom for me is when we live to serve the purpose which we were called to do. We can have campaigns, others may fight our freedom or people may sign treaties to increase the price they paid for our natural resources, as long as we use the gain for ourselves, the country, the continent, will remain unclothed. If in our mind the cause of our miseries is others, then others will do the same and the same and the same to ensure everything remains the same. But if we see the change as inherent to us, then if each of us does something, day by day, the change will reach the four corners of the land and only then we will see the price of our e sacrifice, which in fact is the freedom we seek.

Examples like these are many and we will bring them along so all will see the extent to which our way of life is the cause of our failure, and not only the fact that we sell our resources for cheap. Yes, along the way I will point to our way of life so we know that the mess we are in is not alone down to others, but that we are also the cause of our demise since 50 years and more.

Chapter 7:

We have all we need, now we need all it takes to be ourselves

We mourn in common, hate together, criticise alike and beg shamelessly as we run around barking like dogs to alert the world of our miseries and lack of food; and once we have, we eat at once like there is no tomorrow, to meet the needs of the present. When it is over we start again, day by day without thinking about the future.

Yet it is easier and better for us to come together to produce what is required to meet our needs of now and for the future, and by so doing, we'll be more than able to stand as high as those we accuse, thereby earning the respect we deserve.

Only then will we act like equals and sell our resources at a price we want, because by then we will not be urged by hunger or needs for now; and this will make our kids proud of our endeavours as we would have given them the best they deserve through our work and selfless thinking.

We can be what we want, not necessarily like others, only when we know what we are worth. Although we can copy, it'll only be when this can help us to benchmark against what we are offering, thereby pointing to the difference, which will add more value to our offerings.

Our gold and mines and gas and fuel alone will change
no one, if no one dares to change his mind-set. Our mines
and gold and fuels and gas have always been there and the
price we take will shrink and shrink as long as we care less
for those ahead, and plan only on a day-to-day basis to fill
our needs for now. Because our urge commands the price,
buyers aware of our urges for now, will offer only the
pennies that calm us down, so as to create a state of mind
that links us to them, and to get a repeat of business on
the same terms. This is the law of the market! The law of
supply and demand! As we start as losers without a plan,
so it will remain as long as we care less to question our way
of life. The state in which we find ourselves is created by us,
so long as we ignore the causes of our present down falls,
pushing the blame to others, the more we will sink and
sink until we drown; if we are not already at the bottom
of the water. But we need to remember that wherever we
find ourselves, at bay or at the bottom of the water, there
is always a predator to finish our rest. Therefore it is better
for us to die on our terms than pretend to find peace when
everyone around is looking for where to strike.

The heroes, our true heroes, will stay alive forever, in
our memories for generations, rain or sunshine, despite
the writings that forge history or poison our minds to
think they wronged us. However, no matter what picture
the media may paint, or opinions may hold, oh! Rather
what their opinion may sell, the cube is perfect and always
stands upright. Our cube – the truth – only the truth, but
only the truth will change not and stand still despite the
pushing and rolling and punching. Yes, whoever has senses
to judge will know and doubt not the reasons behind the
fighting all around Africa!

Today, I say, there is no reason to fight back as it is
better to come together and make together what we need

to live, building together the roads we need as slowly or quickly as we can with the tools we can make ourselves, without exchanges that will bury us or our kids in debt to keep us behind forever and ever and ever. Here, our aptness to copy, in order to make our own, will be an example to follow. Machines are wordless and their heart is easy to read, provided we have opened them with care, losing no parts or organs and piecing them back again with care, repeatedly again and again until we are able to know how they work. From here we will be able to build the same with no need to use what we bought and the name and options we add will be our own. We can have heavy machineries and new technologies of our own, fit for our needs. We just need to know what we want and how they will serve us and put the right brains and resources in charge to work at it.

This is the time to choose the brains that we commit to do the finding in the calm, far from worries of the stomach so, their minds are rested and focused to dig, and dig, and dig until they find the secret. This secret we will use, to fill the voids and bring to the market new products, equipment and tools useful to the world, starting with our own. I am sure, like the cube, no kicking or rejection will hide the fact that we are using our findings to meet our needs without the need to beg or buy the same forever, or rent, or lease for more than they are worth. I see a Doctor–professor with ideas, crying and begging for funding to bring his brain child to life, but no one seems to care; at the time, he is ridiculed for his long crayon and I hear the words: Like these…".Do we eat the crayons?" This stupid question reflects our ignorance of the usefulness of research, without which the world will stand still. Many will die without new discoveries, and the world with its resources would release no potential if not for research, Yet in Africa, we put no money into the pot reserved for research. As a developing continent, research should have been our priority and should get the best chunk of our budget.

How come we see no value for such an important area that can help to lift us above the crowd? This lack of emphasis on research further point to our short-sightedness, reflecting our focus only on the present. The now is running past and tomorrow is already at hand, where we will still be here to see the days we thought we'd never see. To see tomorrow as far off is taking the measures from our nose to eyes! Shame on us! Yes, we are still here and we will be here to see this new child grow and graduate. This lap of time would have been necessary to lift ourselves out of the poo. Hellas! We stayed there crying and mourning and organising our pity party together and accusing others of being the causes of our sorrows. There already we learn no lessons and continue making the same mistakes or living the same illusion; thinking we are clever, we deny ourselves the prospect of making our marks. The cars we buy, to make the best of them we change and change parts to use as we need. Why not make the whole as we need it? Is it too hard? No, I am sure, the lack of help or support hinders our efforts to bring such things to life. I mean support from those who are able, yet it takes only a pen and paper coming together to decide the gain for each of us. But with greed looming and jealousy chanting added to the blindness that guides and command our moves, we refuse to support those who can make us gain together.

Now here is the plan, or better, my vision, to harness the best in our people, who are our only priceless resource to build our future in common. New initiative at a local, national and regional level where people can put money together to make what is necessary for the country. In the other hand, we see our prions eating our budget, we didn't invent them and we don't have to keep the same system. We can change the way our prisons work by suspending the prisons and using the guilty to work for free in order to pay for their upkeep, whilst giving something back to the country in keys sectors that will produce more revenues for our countries and those prisoners, free from lockup will become useful to themselves and to the country. With guards watching to deter them from running, they can work rather than waste in prison. For those for whom the prison can help as a resourceful or peaceful place to think, we can accommodate such, provided their discoveries are useful to the country.

There no point in shouting and chanting that Africa is best or rich when all it has is given for free to the benefit of those we chose and voted to do the best, who turned out to be the beasts, who day by day sell for less just to meet the needs of few, or worse, keep a place where they stay without control. It is better to work with us, the mass, despite the threats; for all to know we died in action for the sake of those for whom we care and who deserve to know the truth. Apart from the wonders of the past, our generation has nothing to show to the world, yet more than ever before, we have the tools to stretch our minds and bring the wonders from within that will mark our presence and give a sign that we were once here at this time. If we continue like this, we will create a blank page in the books of history. Yet in the mind of each of us the need and urge to mark history yawn and cry aloud. Only if we could stop a moment, to give attention to these commotions, we could care at least to follow a gentle voice of the spirit within that is pointing to the way in which we can make this happen.

Far within and beneath our minds, He is shouting aloud that nothing is impossible to he who believes. He is showing around examples of people like us, with one head, two hands like us and, perhaps, with bodies impaired, who through self-belief brought about something extraordinary that the world marvels at, and which, in general, we look at and enjoy with the pride that our race is strong and able. As we see and enjoy these marvels, it is only wise to try and do alike in the areas we know, that we like and with which we can mark the world in our own way. The fear of failure or shame of what they may say is one of the biggest strongholds on our ego, which brings nothing but ineptitude. We cry and say we are able. I agree, but shall we be judged by our act or deeds? We say, and chant our faith. I agree, we have faith, but what shall we be judged on? Our faith without works! I am sure as long as the world remains; there is no one without faith. Faith in failure is faith, after all; it shows our worth or instead our works, that we are believing and working to fail. As long as the world remains, there is faith, otherwise we would beg and we wouldn't receive. With faith, we believe in aid, with faith we ask and receive to cover the needs of now and start the same tomorrow. With faith we make children, that they will take care of themselves like the birds of the air or the lilies of the field and so they do, despite the misery and early death, they lived, at least for a moment and with chance, if there is any, they strive and some copy our ways of life, if not all of them. With faith we wake up in the morning, with faith and all our minds, we believe that someone somewhere holds our fate. That someone somewhere blocks our moves, and so we stay put, or stand still. With faith we believe that the world is not fair, yet we do nothing to investigate what the better off have done to be where they are. With faith we drink, and live for now, and deeper within we are sure to enjoy. With faith we claim that tomorrow will take care of itself. With faith we believe that we can't act, as the weight of the world is resting on our shoulders and that any move of ours will cause a crash or they will not let us do it. And our faith works, because we claim the loss before we start and surely we lose. If we go into battle in fear, the enemy will have no trouble in winning. He knows our state of mind and shouts the type of noise he knows will make us jump.

What I am saying? That our faith, since we lack it not, should be used in such a way that we see the results we want. We should have faith to win, and surely we will win. We should have faith to be the best; if this is our will, we shall be. We should have faith to come up with a better way of life. If this is our plan, it will work. We need to have faith in ourselves. If we truly believe, nothing will stop us. We need to have faith in our potential, we need to have faith that the work of our intellectuals, researchers will be used and celebrated across the globe. If we believe, it will be unto us according to our faith. We need to believe we have the best country, the best people, and a bright future. Do we really believe? We need to start believing that all things are possible to any human being and that anything we put our minds to, we can achieve. We need to believe that what is within, in our imagination, can materialise if we wish and work at it. Who has been to the moon? A human being? How did that start, by seeing themselves travelling to the moon? Today we can build under the water, fly, phone, and see in real-time people who are far away.

How did this happen? The thoughts of men. So why are we afraid? If we try and fail, we can try again, and fail, and try and fail and try until we win. If we dream small, we achieve little, if we dream big, we achieve more, but who is noticed is he who dreams big and achieves his dream. We say loud and claim everywhere, what is already known without doubt is that the first man was born here. It is true and has become trivial, we did a lot in the past, yes again, but what has happened to our generation today? People have used our minds to bring us down but, in reality, we are the ones limiting ourselves. The greatest battle is the battle of minds. If we give up, we will be stamped on. If we shut the eyes of our minds or cut the hands of our minds we are surely limbless and therefore powerless. I hear people say, Jesus studied in Egypt, Egypt was great, and Moses married a black woman, Obed-Edom was a Kush – a black person. Yes, Jesus studied in Egypt or at least he grew up there for some time; Moses was raised by black people; the pharaoh, his wife was black; and Obed Edom was black, or better, a man of colour. This is all true. But has this evidence fed our children? Those of the past in Egypt didn't just talk the talk, they lived by example and this is why we know of them today. What have we done? Shall we then all live in the past, feed in the past? Wasn't Portugal great as well? Didn't they explore the world? Wasn't Spain first one time? How much do we hear of their talk nowadays? They lived in their ivory towers and the world fought and overtook them. What standard are we using today? In fact, there were many great civilisations in the past. Babylon, Assyrians, Romans, Greek, African.

Most of these have been destroyed and the world goes in circles, and those who make the best marks write their names in the history. It is as simple as this. If we want to remake history, let's leave our marks today, otherwise, we will still be known to our sons and daughters as a sleeping generation. We could be known for our belief in fate. Known for our lack of plan, our lack of will, we will be known, known for doing nothing. Known for selling our lands cheap! We will be known. Known for begging a lot! We will be known. Known for fighting amongst ourselves! We will be known. Known from running away from our responsibilities! Known for shifting the blame! Known for living for now and helping ourselves at will! From the common wealth once we have our way.

Don't worry; it is not our end yet. This is just a wakeup call. We have a lot to give and have brains to think. Provided we accept the call, nothing can stop our move. As long as we know our destination, the wondering about a waste of time may last, but not for eternity; and a day will come that we raise our hands and voice to say… "At last, at last we have taken our place. It is a new dawn and we have a plan, a plan that involves us all, to act at once at last. Like one, but yet each one apart, unique with one's own mind; whereby coming together, we create our path in common and this will leave our traces in this part of the world and beyond, as a sign to the future, that at last we made up our minds, to put our faith in ourselves in order to free our land from what had robbed our pride, and which made us live in despair." I have a plan, I am sure it's a plan you would like to see come to light in the time of your living, before you pass away, it will be here, for our kids to enjoy, and further for theirs to do the same. This plan is inside here in the space we call our plan… Yes, the plan you see below! This is what we want the most, to leave our marks on earth and to implement our plan. This plan starts with our move forward. What some may call development, because development is inherently part of our very essence! We moved from Stone Age to technological era. I suggest that what we needed the most, right after the independence was a better plan for our common future! A plan for our development; this is what we still need now and we want it the most, more than ever before.

Chapter 8:

What we want the most

What we want is to change for the better, to move forward, and do well. What we want is to live and exercise our true potential whilst acting like we were supposed to act. Acting like able humans, acting with pride and reflecting our true nature. Our nature is to excel, to reflect abundance; after all, we are powerful and reflect the nature of God. If we are made in his image, and we are, we should do as He would do because nothing is impossible. We will therefore break the boundaries of impossibilities. As we break the record for our past achievement, we set a new one. This is in essence what we call progress. Our physical and societal progress should work in tandem with freedom of minds. I mean that social progress will follow our freedom of minds. Progress is also when we are coming out of the shell to enjoy what we have in order to make progress, because progress is the essence of life. Where there is life, there is progress and there is no greater quest in human life than perpetual search for improvement; the quest to do things better, the quest to find new ways of improving our living conditions.

Our imagination is bound by the desire to shed light on problems, to find solutions to difficult tasks, difficult problems and tackle issues that prevent us from living fulfilled lives. The perpetual movement towards newhorizons is what we call progress. This is why, in science, it is agreed that what seems true today may be considered tomorrow as our mistakes, but we must first go through the testing of today's realities to uncover new ways of doing things. But if we are satisfied with where we are today, we are surely jeopardising our future. Progress is the march forward which can be considered as development. We move from one stage to another but as a child grows, we may not instantly see how his height changes, we may not see the face growing, but we see the result. This is an internal movement. The child who is three feet today will soon be four and subsequently mature and this will be seen through his/her physical appearance. Scientists have produced slow motion cameras that can show us how this transformation happens, though we may not see it with our natural eyes. Different stages of growth of any living thing are called development. This term has also been used to measure the progress within our society and how our community goes from one stage to another.

Development is used to assess or qualify how well a country meets its inhabitants' needs. Most used politically, it helps to differentiate countries that use more advanced technologies for the welfare of its citizens. We have developed and developing countries, which means wealthy countries and poor countries. So why are some countries so poor and other so advanced? Some people tell us that where people have the power to choose their government, they are more likely to develop quicker. Although this may be true in certain respects, my questions will seek to answer to the contrary.

Does a country need to be democratic to develop? Is the democracy necessary for development? In other terms, is it possible to become a great nation under an autocratic or tyrannical government? We can say that this happened in Russia, however, these terms are not acceptable and we will not use them today to justify the action of others; therefore, let us ask the question which can be politically acceptable and which corresponds to our orientation in this book. Can a country progress well when one president rules for a long time without sharing power? This is to say in Africa, where we tend to have the same president for years and years. Can we move beyond poverty with presidents who have served for nearly half of a century? My answer will be yes. We can progress in this situation, we can do well, it all depends how we feel mentally and how we plan our move to the top. Can Africa do well, can Africa develop without democracy? Is it possible for an African country to become a great country without regular change in leadership? Do people vote in UAE? I doubt it, but do they enjoy what they have? I think so.

They are a modern example of how democracy alone should not be considered as precondition for development. The development is where there is wealth for citizen to share and where citizens can easily meet their needs for food, shelter, health, production and reproduction without a lot of difficulties. It is where citizens can easily have money to buy experiences they desire. For example with money they can by the experiences of good food, good holiday, good hospital treatment, decent accommodation etc.

These experiences do not necessarily require an elected government or regular change in government. In fact some changes can hinder these experiences and limit people's possibilities to thrive. What people really want is the type of governments that encourage creativity, investment, and freedom of undertaking, freedom of entrepreneurship, and freedom of ambitions! Democracy helps, but not always and we need to understand that what we call democracy is the acceptation of the rules we have agreed upon at the beginning pertaining to the conquest and preservation of power. Democracy is not the government of people by people. The majorly never and has never controlled anything anywhere. The majority is just helping the few to achieve their ambition of power and control. The few that rule the world use manipulation, tactics, lies and money to buy and control experiences of power and wealth. Therefore, it is difficult for poor people to take and control power. This is why it is better to have a thriving nation where many are better off, so they can have more say in the way they are ruled, or at least do best what they are skilled at doing and let those who want power exercise it. People become interested in politics, particularly in Africa, because they see politicians as those who will solve their problems; yet politicians will never do it. We don't care whether people stay in power for a hundred years, what we care for is our people's ability to experience their freedom from within, to participate in the growth of their country whilst enjoying the benefits of the riches endowed by Mother Nature.

Our mind-set is what will make us rich or poor. We can become a rich nation even in autocratic government, provided this government is stable. Where there is instability, there is risk of chaos and when there is chaos, possibilities are limited. But if we have a stable government, even if it is ruled by one person for years and years, and if people are free to undertake their economic activities, the nation will prosper.

We can change governments every year, but as long as we have the same mind-set, we will remain poor. A government is as rich as its people. The government makes money from citizens and if the citizens are poor, the country will be poor and as a result, the government will be poor.

Change sometimes can be a source of destabilisation. Libya and Iraq teach us a lesson. How long will it take for Libya or Egypt to recover? Therefore, the only change we will embrace is the orderly one. The one planned and managed with care. We do not support any change that will bring us back to chaos; the only change we want is the one that will take us forward. This is not to say that change in government shouldn't exist. This should be on our terms, not on other people's terms and we are not pleading for anarchy. In fact, if there is no government, we will fall into anarchy and our possibilities will lessen because peace and stability are necessary for progress. We don't care if the same president is there for 100 years I say it again, provided there is improvement in our living conditions. We want the economy to vibrate; we want money to flow, bounce and stay in our hands. We want our citizens to change their mind-set from oppressed to free, from victims to victors, from beggars to donors. This can only happen when we implement a holistic change. Change in government alone will bring nothing major unless this change is followed by a clear and radical shift to existing systems. This is called revolution. If we were to have a revolution, we would need a revolution that will carry our people so that when the leader is gone, the momentum continues, but if the revolution is based on one person, the risk is even greater. We have seen people shaking the whole country for one or two years and after their departure or death, it became difficult for the country to find its way back to normality.

Incremental change is therefore better because we will move whilst spotting areas of weakness, improving along as we move forward. It takes time but it is sure. With incremental change, we have time to unfreeze, change and refreeze as proposed by Kurt Lewin. The Unfreezing stage is about getting ready to change. It involves getting to a point of understanding that change is necessary and getting ready to move away from our current comfort zone. The more we feel that change is necessary, the more urgent it is, the more motivated we are to make the change. Unfreezing and getting motivated for the change is all about weighing up the 'pros' and 'cons' and deciding if the 'pros' outnumber the 'cons' before you take any action. This is the basis of what Kurt Lewin called the Force Field Analysis.

When I speak to my fellow Africans we all come to the same conclusion, that change was necessary. There is never a better time. We should have changed long time ago and it is still time to change. We just need people like us to create a general dissatisfaction of the current system. I am talking about the change that starts with creating dissatisfaction within. An internal, psychological and spiritual change! This first 'Unfreezing' stage involves moving ourselves, or a particular sector or the entire country or continent towards motivation for change.

The Kurt Lewin Force Field Analysis is a useful way to understand this process and there are plenty of ideas of how this can be done. What we all want is to change and we shouldn't delay any longer. We need to start planning together, without delay and now is time. In my view begging is not the solution and pretending we are poor just to get handouts reduces our ability to realise our potential. We are able and we have a lot to give, after all, it is better to give than to receive. Let's start taking responsibility, or rather, lets us learn to solve our problems by ourselves. This is also a step forward in our mental revolution. We have all we need; we just need to do what is required to be where we ought to be. This requires a will power, the will to change, the zeal for progress and development and a vision to drive us is required. This will be the first thing in our plan together. The new planning of our countries, our infrastructures, our education and administrative system will be our first priority. In fact, we need a plan for a new continent

Michel Ngue-Awane

Part Two:

Our Plan Together Here and Now

Chapter 9:

Ending aid and pity parties

Many African people always pretend to be poor and by pretending they become progressively poor. Must people do so as a sign of humility, but through their confession, they become poor indeed. For me, instead of pretending, it is better to say nothing. We need to acknowledge that we are wealthy if truly we want to enjoy what we have. Poverty is a psychological and spiritual problem. Poverty is in our minds, it starts there and the physical appearance is only the consequence of what we already have in mind. Most of our governments factor aid into their yearly budget. What a shame. How can we plan ahead with a beggar's mentality? This is even shameful when we know quite well that our lands have been endowed with unquestionable wealth.

We also recognise that our people are capable, what is required is just a bit of motivation. Our children should be trained to become independent, and this starts with giving them a sense of responsibility. If nothing is impossible to he who believes, it is appropriate to ensure that our future generations are trained to be solution bringers. We should believe that even in the desert, we can bring water to irrigate and grow crops. Instead of giving food to people, we should train them to grow their own. Instead of dumping them with solutions to their problems, we should help them find the best way to solve their problems.

Each person has within themselves solutions to their problems, the most difficult thing is how to articulate them, but with a little motivation, encouragement and belief, they will, in time discover and propose the best way out for themselves. So what shall we say about aid? Shall we help those who are poor? My contention is that human beings are able. Only a little child requires spoon-feeding and when he is able to fend for himself, he is able to adapt and find solutions to his problems. Yes, some guidance may be required but when we become a solution ourselves, we stop their ability to think, thereby hindering their natural drive to find solutions. Yet, we were put in the world to bring solutions, to cultivate, multiply, replenish and subdue. Each of us has this ability.

I therefore see foreign aid for food as a means to keep ourselves in the state we are in. When we get used to receiving, it becomes difficult to act as able problem solver. We point the fingers toward others and most of all towards our politicians, because we see them as those who should solve our problems. We think that they are grasping all that we have, even though we may have never paid taxes. We cry out loud and push them to beg for us and when they get a bit, they pick a little and dump crumbs on us; this helps us for a day or so and we start the same tomorrow, and day by day we live and want to live on handouts that are far from solving our need.

I am not saying that politicians have no faults of their own, nonetheless, they are needed and each of us can do something for our self. We shouldn't hold a grudge against politicians because without them we would fall into anarchy and this would reduce our ability to thrive. We shouldn't wish to remove people from power by force or war; this alone can create conditions that are worse than the previous and reduce our abilities to achieve what we aimed to do. This has been seen in Iraq and Libya. The population should always be alert and understand when change is possible, but change should not bring chaos. Our actions should be guided by love and our aim should be to increase riches for ourselves and our country. This cannot be done in a lawless state; even when this is possible, those who have such wealth will live in fear and uncertainty.

Most of the time, if not all the time, the pictures we see from Africa or of Africa paints the state of suffering and poverty which warrant the help of the world, and day by day, we beg and receive and beg again and again until we become dependent on aid. We plan our year with aid that we will receive and plan to eat the same and ask for more and year by year, we do the same. It is true that in a state of poverty, there is no way we can provide the love and care we want for our families and those into whom we should be pouring our love; for this, it is only trivial for me to say that love is denied expression by poverty, the spirit of poverty is the reason why there are some atrocities we see today in our land.

But there is no reason we should be so poor to the point that we lack food. Instead of finding solutions to our problems, we become engaged in competition, each of us competing to get what we think is scarce, and this change of focus takes us away from searching within to find the best way to fulfil our need. It is, however, not true that other people's riches will necessarily prevent us from having enough. There is enough in the world to feed the world and there will always be enough in the world to meet the needs of living souls. There is enough in Africa to meet the needs of Africans and even, if need be, the needs of the world. This does not exclude our ability to exchange or buy a variety of things we may want that are produced elsewhere. This is the nature of human beings; the quest for diversity, which is the source of enrichment for all humans.

Resources abound in the world and many are those not yet discovered, perhaps because we don't even know their importance now and we also don't know yet if we will need them. When their needs arise, we will discover and use them. History tells us that when one resource is used up, we will discover the next one to meet the needs of its time, and when it is finished new ones will be found and so on. The world is rich; yesterday we used coal, which was as precious as gold. Today it is the sun we turn into electricity and our black gold has become a liability, unclean energy, and we are condemning countries that use it; tomorrow new methods and resources will be used as our needs for those resources arise. But if we plan on begging to live, we will never be able to meet our needs as long as the world remains, even though there is enough for all to use. I can't think that Neolithic or Palaeolithic man was a beggar.

The Neolithic man did not live or rely on international aid. I have not seen anywhere in history that people lived on handouts and aid a part from people of our generation. Every book that I have read so far presents men as a capable being always in search of betterment and improvement. He went from Stone Age to Iron Age and so on. What he lacked, he got it by exchanging what he had. So why did we suddenly turn into amorphous and useless souls? This is also part of our subconscious programming.

Once our lands were hijacked, the pity party started and people told us that they were sorry for us, for our way of life and for the lack and they imposed on us what they are and a culture of dependence. We then waited for them to do things for us and, throughout the years, our quest to find solutions was disabled. Unconsciously we thought people were doing us good. This is far from the case. Imagine a husband who conditions his wife to become a receiver: he provides everything, solves every single issue she has, electricity, food, etc., for years. It will come to a point where the wife will become unable to think. She will become useless. So have we been conditioned? To wait for the west to bring solutions to our problems and they certainly bring solutions that they want. They tell us how to run our institutions, they tell us what to eat, they tell us what to grow, they tell us which organisation we should adhere to, they tells us what sort of government we should have, they decide what sort of aid we should have and how it should be used and they pity us and tell us they will always be on our side to help when we need them, yet as we know, the aid they give can never set us free.

If we are free, we will no longer depend on them and if we become equal, they stand to lose a lot. So the pity party is serving someone's interests. As human beings, we should understand that we are free and rid ourselves of the fear of impossibility. If we claim to be equals, we should act as equals, knowing quite well that whatever they do, we can also do it. If others are not begging, we are also able to meet all our needs by ourselves. The world is full of resources and we have not even discovered all that we need today because we are not all living to our full potential.

What we need to use is ready and awaits our discovery. We need to work and think on how and what is needed and plan the way we are going to get it. We should completely remove from our minds and plans the need for aid as a way to meet our needs. Aid is a weapon of mass destruction, and I have already said that the greatest battle of our people is not of flesh, but the one we need to fight in our minds.

The poor do not need charity or aid. Aid is for those who have faced extreme natural catastrophe and this should be limited to their immediate needs, just to relieve the situation and give them a breathing space. Yes, just for a short period. Giving those we call the poor a loaf of bread cannot solve their problem. Rather, it keeps them where they are by making them forget for a moment their needs, but these needs resurges just after they have finished eating; and as you keep giving, you keep bringing them down and help perpetuate their misery and poverty for ever and ever. All charities tends to perpetuate the aims of the cause that it wants to eradicate. We rather need to give the picture and state of wealth in the minds of poor people, instead of giving them bread. Charity is just an entertainment, but if we can all prove to poor people that they can be what they want to become, and help them with advice and motivation, if we prove to the poor that they can be rich and that they have the ability become better off and free from poverty and suffering, they will eventually become rich if they accept and believe it.

Wherever we find ourselves, we can create everything we need to live comfortably. We can grow enough cotton and silk, and produce more milk, fish and meat and food than we need to feed all our citizens and beyond. The only thing is that we have not dedicated our efforts to doing so. No one was created to suffer or to fail, poverty or wealth is a direct result of how we apply our knowledge and the way we do things. This starts from the way we think and believe. Poverty starts from our mind; it is the product of our thoughts. James Allen quoted the Bible by saying that as a man thinketh, so is he. This is true. I mean that if we want and believe we can be rich and developed, we will surely be. We have to do things in the way rich and successful people do. It is true that all may not know how, but we have the duty to train and motivate our citizens in this way rather than making them believe they are poor and the country with them.

When we reduce our citizens or make those to whom we should have given hope believe they are poor, when we start asking for charity on their behalf, they subsequently believe that they are poor and fall into this trap, which makes industries that are created to eradicate poverty prosper in business.

Poverty agencies are businesses that want to remain in operation and to remain so, they need customers and their customers are those they call the poor. If there are no poor, they will go bankrupt; therefore, it is not in the interests of those working in these organisations to eradicate poverty. Their hidden agenda or unconscious agenda is to perpetrate and maintain poverty as long as possible so they can prosper. My view is that help against poverty should come from somewhere else instead of those who declare themselves fighting against it. In my view, help should come from individuals labelled as such. Poor people themselves should be encouraged to find solutions to their demise. They have within themselves the right solutions. Life coaches don't impose or teach anything to their clients. They encourage them to bring out what they have within themselves, and guide them to structure it. So the so called poor people should be life-coached. Similarly, it is never and will never be the will of aid agencies to go bankrupt or go out of business; those who work within this industry earn a living and it is their prime aim to keep and secure their income by justifying their existence.

The money managed by aid agencies could easily be used to create conditions in which people's needs are met in the long term, but what will happen to those who earn big salaries in these agencies when their aim is accomplished? Countries who give need to maintain an upper hand, a way for them to keep the needy down and dependent. This helps them justify their dominance and superiority. They would become redundant if there were no poverty, and who wants to be seen or considered as useless?

We need to help people to acquire the ability to think positively, to think of possibilities and to self-value. We need to train them to think in terms of what they want to be and to think positively and of possibilities; basically, to know how great their potential is. Spinoza suggested that the more things the mind knows, the better it understands both its own powers and the order of nature. Now the better it understands its own powers, the more easily it can direct itself and lay down rules for its own guidance; and the better it understands the order of nature, the more easily it can restrain itself from useless pursuits, and can understand that an idea is situated in the context of thought exactly as is its object in the context of reality.

To think that they are rich and able to produce and reproduce what they require and live fulfilled lives is the way poor people should be motivated to think. To think that there is abundance all over the world and that everyone can have unlimited access to the world's treasury is what is required of the poor, not charity. Some people, basically a few people, have prevented anyone from getting what they need by spreading the rumour that resources are limited. This is not true and the world is still in construction as I have already said. This is why yesterday's technologies become obsolete today and new things are created and discovered and invented. Those who create and invent are human beings, and have not become creative inventors by preventing anyone else doing it, but they have become so through dedication, devotion, belief and working towards their goals.

We create our conditions by our thought process and we can only change them through our thought process. Anything that has ever been made started with an idea before materialisation, and poverty is more a mental attitude than physical. People may have a lot of wealth, but still be poor or live in poverty. I have seen individuals who die in derelict conditions just for people to discover that they had a lot of savings after their death, and those who inherit such wealth will soon become poor if they have not prepared their minds for wealth.

It follows that our independence did not change our conditions because we perceived independence as a physical condition rather than a psychological condition, and this is why, even though physically no one occupies our lands today, we are still under the thumb of the imperial and colonial powers. If we had prepared our minds for ultimate spiritual freedom, we would have been free by now. Once our mind is set free, we are free indeed. This process is still possible through a process of reprogramming of our subconscious.

It is unfortunate that we saw our independences as a physical condition; we thought that by chasing the colonising power away, we will be in charge, ignoring that their plans were firstly spiritual before their materialisation into physical systems that were implemented. We failed to spot the traps and we failed to dismantle the colonisation of our minds.

We always say that they came with guns, the Bible and

the carrot. This was planned long before and implemented progressively during their settlement to the point that, after the independence, we had no choice but to feel that we needed them. We surely needed them because we were navigating in a system where we were complete strangers. The only way we would have gone on without them was to review things and implement our own systems and strategies, based on our values, our plans and vision. Since we did not have any vision of our own, we moved with other people's vision and the result is that we still ended up depending on them. It is not surprising that, soon after the physical occupation, we found ourselves going back to those we said were bad for our future, only for them to determine what future we should live from then on. We looked at visible supplies rather than thinking and looking at unlimited supplies that have always been and will always be found in our immediate environment.

In the early nineteen fifties and sixties, few of the mines and gold and portfolio of what has been discovered in Africa today had been exploited; yet people were able to develop and become great using the resources we took for granted and worthless. We chased them away without mastering what to do with these resources and without knowing what we could do with them. We soon were running after them to come back and get them cheaper, basically for peanuts, and did not stop to think which other resources could be found and what we could do with them. They returned again, and discovered, and told us what they could do with them and took them on their terms. We called them in again and again to explore and see if they could find new things, without attaching any condition that protects us, and we soon found out that new resources were discovered and that we had been fools to give them away for nought. We can succeed and develop with what we already have or what we can find in our environment and it will be impossible for us to move a foot higher if we continue to put ourselves down and turn always to the outside world to meet our needs.

There are always possibilities seeking expression through human beings and poverty is not part of God's original intent for men. If we can just but stop to think that what we are conceiving in our thoughts is not impossible, we will win the battle against poverty. We can be free and prosperous if we want and believe without doubt.

We are used to tales, and this has lured us into all sorts of fictions to the point that we have relegated our destinies to chance; hoping that things will happen or that our conditions will change perchance or a genie will appear and fix the situation at once. We therefore take aid and hope that this aid will one day change its nature and that, by some benefactor's goodwill, we will suddenly become wealthy and successful. If this was to happen as suddenly as we imagine, we would not be able to handle it because success is when preparedness meets opportunities. We may have gold but if we don't know what it is or what to do with it, it will still mean nothing to us.

Spinoza said that the less the mind understands while yet perceiving more things, the greater its capacity to form fictions; and the more it understands, the less its capacity to form fictions. When we understand our true human nature and the power we have within us to make things happen and decide our own destinies, we will understand why believing and faith precedes actualisation and achievement. In our mind, we must understand that we are able to create better conditions for ourselves through careful planning and focus, because what cannot be obtained by chance can be obtained by careful planning.

Spinoza continued that when we know the nature of a

body, we cannot entertain the idea of an infinite fly; or when we have come to know the nature of the soul, we cannot entertain the idea that it is square; our contentment and dependency comes from the fact that we wilfully engaged in and accepted fallacies as true as a result of our laziness or lack of self-assessment. And this in turn reduced us to the same level as those who have no mind or have lost their minds, or those who live without knowing why they are alive. Yet we have been created for a purpose and we cannot continue to be consumers, receivers and beggars.

We have to express our true nature, realise our potential, reject handouts as this furthers our dependency and reduces our abilities to stretch ourselves beyond our present circumstances. It is clear as Spinoza says, that "the less men know of their nature, the more easily they can fashion numerous fictitious ideas, such as that trees speak, that men can change instantaneously into stones or springs, that ghosts appear in mirrors, even that gods can change into beasts or men, and any number of such fantasies". At this time it looks like we are still living in these fantasies. We think that suddenly, by an act of a genie, we will overcome our present situation without any effort and planned action. Any results that come unexpectedly are only a result of banked efforts. If results were to be random, and if this was to happen as suddenly as we think, we would not know how to handle recognise it. Perhaps, we have already missed plenty of opportunities that we did not recognised as opportunities, just because we were not prepared for them. Through conscious efforts, we learn how to master issues and the more we learn to master them, we build our ability to handle and manage them.

We cannot succeed by turning all our hopes, wants and

needs over to outsiders. We cannot succeed if we continue to depend on foreign nations. Aid and gifts will never set us free. We need to understand that the sort of aid we receive is debts and we are rich enough to help ourselves as well as others.

Africa should be helping the west, if we organised ourselves and used our resources properly. It is not enough to have lands and resources. The principal thing is to use them well. I have travelled to over 25 African countries and everywhere, people expect handouts, and where people are used to handouts, they stop thinking. I have lived in Europe for years and have personally helped a good number of people who are not better off today than they were when I started helping them.

One person once said to me in the late nineties, "if you give me 300,000 XAF I will never ask you for help again." I gave 500,000 XAF. After two months he was back telling me that the business had collapsed. Yet within the same time, people were rising and doing well in the same business having started with less than 50,000 XAF. Another person in the early 2000s said, "Please help me build this business, I need a million XAF." I gave over two million XAF asking him to reserve some money aside just in case. A year later, I received a phone call. Please Ben, I wouldn't call. Money aside just in case. A year within the same time, people were rising and doing well money you sent was put into a business that collapsed. My reply was this: "Every time you have a problem, you already have a solution because I am the bank and will draw you a blank cheque. If I die today, will you live? I know it will hurt because you will probably miss me, but most certainly you will miss what I provide for you, but will you die with me?" He did not reply, I told him that he was the man to decide his destiny. I have never helped him again and he has since found a way to adapt and to better himself. I am proud of what he has done and he did it because he started counting on his own strengths.

Few will deny that there is a clear moral imperative for humanitarian and charity-based aid to step in when necessary, such as during the 2004 tsunami in Asia. Nevertheless, it's worth reminding ourselves that emergency and charity-based aid cannot help us build a better future. Aid-supported scholarships have certainly helped send African girls to school, but schools that perpetuate a system that we don't like and from where there will be fewer jobs as an outcome. Help and aid are an easy solution, a shortcut, and should not be considered except in the case of emergency, such as natural disasters, extreme hunger, spread of diseases etc. If anything, help should be limited to emergency and advice. Aid that can work is likely to be in the area of capacity building. This should be provided for a limited period of time and, where necessary, should be given to people directly, letting them choose to do what they wish to do. It is not because someone is hungry that he will prefer food now; some people who are hungry will prefer seeds for the next seasons, others will prefer a small capital amount that can help them start something that will generate income. Some people, with cash, can delay their dinner for a day and with money in hand can create a surplus from what they have today for tomorrow's subsistence.

Every day, we hear a story of how much help charities have raised, whether it be millions if not billions a year, and most of this money is donated by citizens and often those who give are not really wealthy. They are touched by the cause and a sacrifice of one meal for something that can save lives. This is Europe. In Africa, there is help too as families rely on family members, but the over-reliance on those who are better off brings everyone down. What makes Europe strive for improvement is that everyone wants to earn for themselves. It is individualist, selfish, but educative. Not that we should all adopt this, but that the spirit of entrepreneurship should be copied and dependency and over-reliance on assistance put aside. Yes, I as said, aid should be used in the case of extreme emergency, not to allow people to eat on a daily basis.

Just as an example, a young man set up a small shop manufacturing and selling mosquito nets in his village and he employed five people and all together they support their families of about 50 people in total. This entrepreneur worked hard to overcome hardship and suddenly a benefactor came to the village and distributed mosquito nets. This benefactor was concerned about people's safety in the village and his gesture was genuine and from his heart. The people from the village were very happy and welcomed the donation provided by the benefactor. From this time, they did not buy mosquito nets, and the mosquito net business that was thriving in the village, employing five people and sustaining 50 people within the employees' extended families, went under because there were no more buyers for the mosquito nets. The owner had to reduce the price of the stock he had left to survive for a few months, and after that, he was out of business. The business closed, five employees lost their jobs, and 50 people were affected, whilst villagers benefited from free mosquito nets for a short period.

After a year, all the mosquito nets given for free were now torn, the village no longer had anyone to supply mosquito nets, their families and dependents suffered hardship because those who were in employment had lost their jobs. The mosquito nets had covered their heads and protected them against malaria for a year, but within this time, they barely had money to meet their daily needs. With no capital, the man who used to make the mosquito nets could no longer start a business, the village had lost a business, hunger and mosquitoes killed more people than before. Mosquito nets sourced from somewhere else became very expensive and unaffordable for people from the village; therefore mosquitoes caused more damage than before the donation. The mosquito nets project was a one off project and has not been repeated; however, the immediate benefits were written off by the negative outcomes caused by this project's long term consequences.

We can see that if the benefactor had instead injected more money into the mosquito nets business to help the owner employ more workers and trainees, the business would have been more sustainable, the price would have reduced as a result of mass production, there would have been more jobs in the village and in a long terms, people would have become less dependent. This example can be transferred into any sector and it highlights the devastating effect of aid in Africa. When people are happy they sit in their office and conceive projects which in their minds are good but they totally ignore the central effect of their charity and their impact on people they want to help.

Evidence of ineffective foreign assistance is widespread all over Africa. The debate on how aid can be effective and contribute to Africa's development should, however, be abandoned altogether. Capable nations are not waiting for people to help them develop. Aid should be turned into mutual cooperation. Working together on useful and important projects rather than waiting for handouts. I have never heard of a country that has developed on aid.

Our goal should be helping ourselves overcome our problems, since decades of foreign aid have done little in changing our destinies. After all, our destinies can only be changed by ourselves. Men are created for a purpose but they are responsible for their destiny. Destiny means destination, where I am heading to, where I am going, where I want to be, where I ought to be. That is my destiny. My destination… as we can see, our destination is up to us. Yes, we may lose focus, and may enter the wrong train or taxi, but when we know where we are going, where we are supposed to be and as long as we are still willing to head there, we will surely arrive.

As I argued earlier, we are created for a purpose and nature always endows us with what we need to arrive at our destination. If our purpose cannot be fulfilled where we are, we will not know where we are supposed to be. Discovering our purpose in life is difficult but once we are clear, we can fulfil it. In poor countries like Niger, Burkina Faso, Mali, Benin, there are billionaires; how did they strive in such an environment? In remote villages of Cameroon, there are people who have never crossed the river leading to the next city, yet they are better off. How did they manage? They applied the principle of wealth creation. No one can be rich by working for someone else or outside of their main area of strengths, nonetheless, everyone has got an area of strengths that needs to be discovered and fostered.

Has Africa discovered its main area of strengths and have we maximised in this area? As long as we continue to sell ourselves cheap, we will be bought at a price we don't deserve.

As a reminder, we are all working for others, developing other countries industries and growing their economies as retailers. We in Africa are selling other countries' goods, exploiting our resources for other nations, sending our children to school to learn other people languages and their system which is replicated in our country, consciously or not. We have no industries of our own, no official languages of our own and all our children are forces to abandon their own languages to speak others people's. Up to 60 years after the independences, we are still not trying to protect our languages. Our minorities' languages are disappearing fast. All our national efforts are put together to make other nations riche because we have nothing attached to our name in the market. In short terms, we are working for other nations. When you work for someone, your wages and earnings are predetermined by that person. Your holidays, your home time, the time you spend with your family, the times you go out and come in are predetermined by your employer. It is clear that we are unconsciously employed by foreign corporations and our earnings are determined by them in the form of profit. Directly or indirectly!

For example, you may cancel a late dinner because you should be at work tomorrow. You may not visit a relative on time because you need to fulfil your obligations. When our petrol and mines need to produce more is determined by others because we are working for them, wilfully but unconsciously. Our conscious mind tells us that we are being fooled, but our unconscious mind commands us to do what we are supposed to do as if we had no choice. If we stop, we will readapt; yes the transition will be difficult but we will adapt and find new ways of living. This ability is inherent to human nature. But why do we continue to go on even though we are so uncomfortable doing so? We certainly lack courage and drive to do so. We need to be resolute if we are to overcome these self-imposed barriers.

To compare our system with aid, I would say that when you depend on handouts, you need to be where they are being distributed, on time; you are preconditioned to wait every end of the month for a handout. This is ture. Even when I help family members, I am never fixed in my pattern of sending money to them because I don't want to condition them to wait for money on a certain day. I may surprise them with a good amount of money and then send nothing for months. This gives them breathing space and freedom to think about how they can meet their daily obligations. Sometimes, I refuse to help not because I cannot but because I want them to maintain their ability to think creatively in search of solutions to their problems and this has worked. People know they can count on themselves and by so doing they are able to adapt and find better ways of meeting their needs. African diaspora is disappointed. I hear stories here and there where money sent for projects has not been used for the intended purpose and how help from families and friends had failed to relieve people back home. This is because the majority of people receiving are not prepared to be solution bringers. Their ability to think is disabled and their expectation has been reduced to the receiving mentality. Those who are prepared are better off because a single penny received is used for sound projects which in turn produce better results.

It is still my contention that aid is playing against us. Aid programmes are counterproductive and annihilating. Aid programmes keep us enslaved and dependent. Evidence overwhelmingly demonstrates that aid to Africa has made Africa's people poorer, and grow slower. The insidious aid culture has left African countries more debt-laden, more dependent and more vulnerable. Amongst all the species, human beings are the only species that can think, imagine and invent. For example, we went from eating raw fruits to cooked meals. We went from using stones to using machetes and, even better, equipment and machines are now used. I have never seen a lion cook his pray, or a monkey, which they say is our closest ancestor, build houses. I have never seeing them cultivating a farm. This ability that is in us as human is enough to help us take charge of our full destinies and work our way out of poverty. Poverty is a spirit, a mentality, and wilful abnegation of responsibilities. Abnegation of our responsibilities towards our offspring and future generations! If no one invented school, medicines or building materials, we would be worse off today. Human beings like us have done it. Yet in Africa, we tend to use and over depend on what will come from the west. We tend to assume that they hold our destinies. That they cannot allow us to develop! Of course they have no interest in doing so. Life is a competition to survive and we are all naturally egoistic.

Everyone is trying to improve their individual conditions and if we do the same, we will somehow meet in the middle. Why do you think rich people don't give you the secret of their trade? Because that is what makes them different and rich! That is what helps them to have competitive advantage. And we all want to be strategically different, better, and possibly be considered as saviours and helpers. This gives us respect and authority. That is one of our basic needs as identified by Maslow, who placed it at the top. Self-actualisation! The "I-have-arrived" mentality that most people have, due to individual's ego. Instead of waiting for others to find a solution for us, we should be the one to strive for it and in so doing, we will find solutions that will benefit us and others thereby making us desirable, needed and useful. The solution to our problem is an open door to another person's difficulties. Yet we may do so without other beneficiaries in mind.

Rich nations want self-actualisation. After they have achieved it, deviously or not, they have gained advantage using what they had at their disposal, be it a trick or force or manipulation. But if we certainly knew our destinations, if we all knew what we stood for and had a bottom line, we would negotiate better, and bargain in a different way.

We can do all things, or rather, nothing is impossible. But if we resign, or think that we cannot do it, we have already limited ourselves, thereby making it difficult to achieve what would have been within our reach. We can find a cure for Ebola, for AIDS, for tuberculosis. They all come from plants and those looking for cures elsewhere are humans like us. This is done by studying the plan, the human nature and virus behaviour… yes; we will say that we need sophisticated machines. Did Europe start with sophisticated machines, were their discoveries perfect at the beginning? And have they been perfected? NO. The nature of science is that today's truths are the lies of tomorrow. Yet we advance it. We need to take a first step and take a second one until we are able to run. But as new athletes, we cannot compete with the likes of Usain Bolt. Yet in 20 or 50 years someone will do better than Usain Bolt. This person could be us if we have remained in the race and are still willing to learn from our mistakes and start the race again.

What have we really done since we claimed our independence? What? A car created….large farms? Better schools? New education systems? Better government system? Better manufactures? New machines? Better hospitals? None of these; we copied and we continue to copy what we know is bad for our future. We still build in the same way. We live in hot countries and have not adopted a code of constructions. We waste energy. I was surprised when I visited Spain. I realised that our constructions are similar to Spanish architecture. The same types of buildings have been erected for over 100 years and we have not tried to come out with new ways of building efficiently. We need to review this sector; in fact we need to review every sector of our social infrastructure. We need to redefine our own standard in every area. Even in sectors like construction it is quite clear that we waste energy and we don't capitalise on all advantages that we have.

We should have built houses adapted to our weather. Who will start the process? We are waiting for the transfer of technologies and we say it and claim it every day. Why would someone who spent millions researching new technologies transfer that to you? And if they do, do you think it will be done for you? No the transfer will be in their terms to maximise their revenues because they have spent their time and money developing it. Instead of fighting for the transfer of foreign technologies we should be aiming at developing our own technologies, adapted and suited for our needs. We should be trying to use our own resources to build what we need. We should design our houses in the way we need, suitable for our weather, hot weather and raining seasons.

All over Africa things look the same. It is like African people all meet to decide how a market should look. How a school should look, how an officer should behave. But on the contrary, in Europe, you know that you are in a different country just by the look of the roads, even though there are no physical barriers. When you look at how houses are built, you know you have crossed the border even from England to Ireland, from France to Luxemburg, from Germany to Switzerland.

Africa should rise above the colonial subconscious, surprise people by changing its mind-set. We should have in mind a road map for our development, count on our people to meet our people's need, use our resources to improve our condition, and each nation should identify what makes them different from others and capitalise on it. Most of all, we should as far as possible detach ourselves from the culture of self-pity, spoon-feeding aid. We should be able to have confidence in ourselves and in our ability to meet the challenges we face. We are now aware that we are not free, and that our tendency to ask for aid had been part of a plan to hold us where we are. Although this is the worse prison one can be in, we can come out at any time without and formal procedures. It is up to us to decide the right moment. Let's start with small steps, let's move on as proud people.

Chapter 10:

Sector-targeted aid works but spoon-feeding aid stagnates

We need to move from spoon-feeding aid to sector-targeted aid. This means that we need to allocate what we would have used normally to feed people, to develop a particular promising sector. Instead of giving food to fight hunger, we can use the money to develop agriculture or for the irrigation of arable lands. In so doing the agricultural sector will, in the long run, become self-sufficient. People will say that aid is important; I say only in an emergency situation. Where in Europe do you see people living and counting on a whole programme of aid? Yes, there are charities, but when it becomes a serious problem like in Africa, the state develops a strategy to deal with the issue. Most aid programmes are around the alleviation of poverty in Africa, yet poverty continues to become more of a problem.

Aid programmes have not reduced poverty, because poverty is not a physical problem. Poverty is a mental issue. I see some houses where people live with the walls and roofs falling, in villages where just a few metres away there is a bush full of straw that could be used to cover the roofs. The soil is there that can be dug to rebuild the wall. These houses did not require sophisticated technologies to build but we let them fall in front of our very own eyes and we cry for help I am baffled. They are mud houses, built by people. Now they are falling, the only effort required is to use the same mud that was used to fortify or rebuild it.

But the poor house remains so for years and when it rains, people are wet in their own houses. Why is this? This is not because in these villages there are no resources to make good shelters. It is because people choose to live this way. We use mud to build houses; when they are disintegrating, we can use the same mud to seal the holes and cracks. We can use leaves for roofs. Houses are pricey in Europe and well maintained, yet we neglect ours and let them fall and cry around that we have no houses or roofs.

There are enough resources in Africa to feed its inhabitants and more. There is in reality no poverty; there is a lack of plan and will. Yes, some people will be weak or sick, but if there is a plan there will be safety nets to help those at risk.

If we had better planning, we would have had better infrastructures. A well organised system is when all parts of the system are interacting and supporting each other. For example a good agricultural system will sustain farmers who will have enough to buy fertilisers and chemical industries producing fertilisers will thrive each gaining the right salary and the company would have enough resources to further research, and better research would help create better industries and the better industries will yield benefits and banks will have confidence in these companies to fund their projects and so on money would be generated in the country meaning g that the country would become richer with it citizens better off.

Instead of getting handouts for food, aid can be used to develop research centres, develop the industrial sector, set up factories, intensive agriculture, aquaculture, livestock etc.

In contrary programmes of aid relive a situation on a temporary basis and the same problem will emerge again. If aid is used to develop research centres, industrial sector, set up factories, carry out intensive agriculture, aquaculture or livestock there will be long terms benefit and the whole system would improve.

Instead of giving chemical products to people to spray their farms, this could be used to set up such factories and sell the product cheap. Develop whatever may be needed in the country, using the people of the country. This is how aid will be effective. Since the independences, and before, Africa had been receiving aid, yet every day, it needs it even more. If we stop and help people to find solutions to their problems, starting by telling them that inside their own minds they have the solutions, they will overcome their self-imposed limitations. The type of aid we have today is worse than weapons used against the same people we are helping because it prevents them from thinking. When they are waiting for the handouts, they do nothing but watch the time and count how much time separates them from their next consignments.

Sector-targeted aid has worked in Europe; farmers get subsidies; most of us don't know this but this is the case. This helps them to develop and try new crops. In Europe, because aids has been geared toward adjusting and pump priming key targeted areas of the economy, it benefits both the funders and the beneficiaries. We have seen this work in the Republic of Ireland in the 1990s when aid played a key role in the transition of the Irish economy right from 1993 to 2007. This aid was provided in the form of structural funds and cohesion funds, targeted at building infrastructure. This is because they needed infrastructure, but for us, we need food on the table and the solution is to have a prosperous agricultural system. We need to intensify our agriculture if we want to overcome hunger. Whilst developing key sectors that are needed, we also need to develop people's minds, not with the present educational system but with motivational programmes that give them confidence that they can and are able to fend for themselves.

If we were to require aid we should ensure that it is targeted at the right sectors. If not, its effects will be extremely damaging because aid has created a culture of dependency on handouts or, even worse, a culture of corruption, whereby proximity to political decision-making and access to the funding that comes from aid has led to the money going in the wrong direction. This in turn has stifled free enterprise, and competitiveness, because it had incentivised people to be politically clever, rather than entrepreneurial and productive.

I have huge admiration for the Bamilikes of Cameroon; they never despair or give up. They don't wait to get jobs in the central administration or public administration and even when they have jobs, they have businesses on the side, whether a shop, a farm, or a service business or import–export. By so doing, they have become the powerhouse of Cameroon's economy and money bounces from one hand to another and mostly bounces into Bamilikes' hands. Money can bounce from Bamilikes to Bamilikes 30 times before it bounces out, and when it does, it goes straight away back to Europe or the USA or China.

The money should be bouncing and staying in the country, but because the country produces nothing, all products that are used transfer our capital to foreign countries. If there were manufacturers, the money would bounce and stay and this would be a great deal for the economy.

In Cameroon for example, money bounces from Bamilikes to Bamilikes because they own:

- grocery stores
- convenience stores
- petrol service stations
- restaurants and bars
- roadside restaurants
- wholesale supply stores
- restaurant supply stores
- hair salons
- nail salons
- shoe stores
- beauty supply stores
- men's clothing stores
- ladies' clothing stores
- children's clothing stores
- print shops
- dress maker shops
- shoe maker shops
- butcher's shops
- bakery shops
- coffee shops
- electronic repair shops
- computer repair shops
- cell phone shops
- bridal shops
- marriage halls for rent including chairs and self-service
- dentists' offices
- medical supply stores
- doctors' offices
- pharmacies
- credit unions

- banks
- laundry shops
- bars
- night clubs
- private schools and training centres
- second hand stores
- taxi firms and car sales
- holiday homes
- construction and building companies
- topographic rental material shops
- housing supply for rent
- transport companies
- cell phone top up services
- internet café services and photocopiers
- bookstores
- laundry
- coffee export factories
- they are porters in the market
- they wash cars
- they repair cars and tyres and they sell parts they lend money with interest

This list is the list of things we need almost every day and these services they offer help them to make money in return. So when a top public servant gets paid, the money goes straight away from their pocket to buy one of these services. It follows that most of the highly paid public workers are poor because they cannot keep their money and the law of money is to have it and keep it as long as we can or at least make it stay in our pockets as long as possible, so money can meet money in our pockets, and in so doing, we have enough to afford things that require a huge amount of money.

In the example above, money bounces from public

sectors workers, and almost any other citizens to a Bamilikes' hand and from one Bamilike' hand to another because from one sector to another, a Bamilike is seller and retailer.

When money bounces and stays in your pockets, you will in the long run have a considerable amount of money to afford better and more important things and this is what we call capital. He who has liquidity has more opportunities. With a great amount of liquidity, you can easily buy a piece of land that is being sold in a rush, you can buy a building that is being sold to solve a problem, and you can acquire a factory that is closing or being foreclosed.

On the contrary, if you have nothing, no one will lend you money and your buying power is reduced. Those who have less, the little they have will be taken away. If you have £10 and you need food, the £10 will go straight away toward your needs and you will have nothing left. This is why it is said that those who have little, the little they have will be taken away from them. You had £10 and for one day food, your £10 has been taken away from you and you are left with nothing. But when you have more, you can acquire more and people can trust you with more, thereby enabling you to afford more things.

The number of businesses above represents the number of times money will bounce from one hand to another hand because they are things that are used by each citizen. In the case of Cameroon with the Bamilikes, money will go from one Bamilikes to another and that is why they hold the key to the economy, so, if they are a united group, they will be even more successful. If there are no public jobs today, they will still live and they will continue as if nothing had even happened; in fact they will become even richer, because those who were working in these sectors will come to them to borrow and they will end up selling them the little assets they have in order to survive.

This happened in Egypt when during the famine, people exchange their livestock, land and all their assets against food to the point that the state became the owner of all lands except the land belonging to the priest. These same people after the famine were working in the lands that once belonged to them, but for a percentage of returns. They became employees and tenants in their own homes and lands. The transfer of their wealth went to the treasury. This just shows how with more you can attract more.

Let's see what happened exactly in Genesis 47 from verse 13 to 25 in the New Living Translation it says: Meanwhile, the famine became so severe that all the food was used up, and people were starving throughout the lands of Egypt and Canaan. By selling grain to the people, Joseph eventually collected all the money in Egypt and Canaan, and he put the money in Pharaoh's treasury. When the people of Egypt and Canaan ran out of money, all the Egyptians came to Joseph. "Our money is gone!" they cried. "But please give us food, or we will die before your very eyes!"

Joseph replied, "Since your money is gone, bring me your livestock. I will give you food in exchange for your livestock." So they brought their livestock to Joseph in exchange for food. In exchange for their horses, flocks of sheep and goats, herds of cattle, and donkeys, Joseph provided them with food for another year.

But that year ended, and the next year they came again and said, "We cannot hide the truth from you, my lord. Our money is gone, and all our livestock and cattle are yours. We have nothing left to give but our bodies and our land. Why should we die before your very eyes? Buy us and our land in exchange for food; we offer our land and ourselves as slaves for Pharaoh. Just give us grain so we may live and not die, and so the land does not become empty and desolate."

So Joseph bought all the land of Egypt for Pharaoh. All the Egyptians sold him their fields because the famine was so severe, and soon all the land belonged to Pharaoh. As for the people, he made them all slaves, from one end of Egypt to the other. The only land he did not buy was the land belonging to the priests. They received an allotment of food directly from Pharaoh, so they didn't need to sell their land.

Then Joseph said to the people, "Look, today I have bought you and your land for Pharaoh. I will provide you with seed so you can plant the fields. Then when you harvest it, one-fifth of your crop will belong to Pharaoh. You may keep the remaining four-fifths as seed for your fields and as food for you, your households, and your little ones."

Pharaoh's servants." We see how those who failed to plan easily lost their wealth and freedom. Even in these circumstances, we don't see joseph or the pharaoh setting up any aid programme. Aid programme in this case would have crippled the country and people would have stopped working, the country would have been worse off after the famine. In the case of Cameroon, it looks like the Bamilikes would do well and would not rely on any aid programmes.

In fact why would they need aid if they are doing so well? They need it less, and this is because they don't sit down and wait for people to solve their problems for them. They understand that public administration cannot solve their problems and by owning businesses they are more valuable to the state than any other groups because they pay taxes and are visible. In fact, they are making the country go forward. They employ people, they develop the country, and they plan ahead. This is what the west has done. They own most of the industries or manufacturers that produce what is needed in the world, and sell what they produce worldwide, and money comes from everywhere to boost their companies as well as their economies; consequently their countries. They can employ more citizens of their countries, pay more taxes and fund new initiatives. They become those who can make or break governments and their respective countries' heads go around the world negotiating deals for them and where there is a resistance, they can forge stories to bring these governments down.

Despite the dynamism of the Bamilikes of Cameroon, the country still loses, but imagine if the country were producing all products that are sold in the land. Imagine if the country were able to produce even half of what is consumed and used in the country. If that were the case, money would bounce over and over and stay as long as possible in the country and more people would become more prosperous, the state would have more in taxes, more jobs would be produced and more people would be inspired thereby moving from the state of poverty to freedom. Imagination and inspiration also come from what we can see but if we have never seen big things, greater things, it might be a struggle to dream big.

The group presented above, the Bamilikes, are only resellers or retailers because they don't produce most of what they sell, and, therefore, what definitely stays in the country is only the profit generated by their transactions. The big chunk of the money is used as capital to buy products for consumption which are not made in the country. The products they buy are not made in the country; therefore they are simply helping other countries make their money. Basically they are working for foreign companies, though unconsciously. They are middlemen and women buying and selling foreign goods, making profits in the process. If we were able to produce most of the goods sold in our markets, we would overcome poverty in no time.

We need to produce most of the small items that we take for granted but which are used for our everyday needs. I have looked at many countries in Africa and realised that the following are not produced locally, yet we use them every day without questioning their origin, hence, most of our local entrepreneurs fail probably to notice that money can be made from these products. We need to produce:

- razor blades and other shaving tools
- own research and most petrol service stations
- hair products including extensions used by women
- nails and shoes
- cosmetic products
- textile companies with the capacity to supply to the whole country and beyong
- children's clothing stores
- utilities companies
- electronic repair shops, air transport companies, sea transport (boats and transit companies, railways, etc)
- Sea transport
- railway transport companies
- computer manufacturers
- mobile phone manufacturers and network companies
- car manufacturers
- medical equipment manufacturers
- banks and credit unions
- national breweries with national brands

- hotels, restaurants, bakeries, leisure centres
- holiday homes, travel agencies, recruitment agencies, accounting and consultancy firms, building maintenance and facilities companies
- road building companies
- heavy machineries and factories to make them
- household goods manufacturers
- health products
- hygiene products
- we need to have farms and engage in intensive agriculture, aquaculture and life stocks
- Bikes, toys, building materials, etc

This list can be expanded and will be expanded when we carry out our needs analysis or inventory to identify what we may need and what we already have, in order to identify the gaps.

We can see how easily most of the things we spend our money on are owned by foreign companies, and this means that we give our earnings to these companies. Our middlemen like the Bamilikes we talked about earlier, help to collect the money for them and make a living as middlemen and women. In reality, they work consciously or unconsciously for those companies. If these companies, like the Chinese, were to enter into competition with them, by retailing their products themselves as they have started doing in most African countries, they would soon be out of the market. The state needs to step in and protect the local economy. It is a dangerous situation because if nothing is done, we will end up in a situation where our citizens are all observers and helpers of other countries' companies.

We need to start local and national companies and manufacturers to produce what we need, so that our money can bounce and stay in the land. If not, we will always be at the mercy of international corporations; thus helping them to collect from here to build somewhere else. It is therefore important for us to act, and act fast. By supporting key sectors, through our sector-targeted aid, we will be able to overcome this handicap. Africa can make most of the things it needs, and collaborate through aid or bilateral agreements in the areas where support is required. This is what is required rather than receiving aid, which so far has only furthered our dependency. If we are able to do this our money will bounce at least 12 times before moving abroad.

Chapter 11:

Mobilising ourselves, using what we have to build what we want

Russia and the eastern bloc were poor at the beginning of the 20th century, but due to self-belief they contributed to the world progress, scientifically, economically and intellectually. Many discoveries were made either by the western or eastern bloc. Infrastructures were developed; technology and agricultural techniques were being used to advance the country. But in Africa, we were dancing and following the leaders, begging for food and pleasing who gave us more. We were neither at the left nor right. We were neither capitalist nor communist, a clever move that would have benefited us if it had been well planned.

We could have seized the moment to develop our research in key sectors of our economy, but instead, we did so to get aid and most of our cooperation was in the area of defence; we had wars here and there, each dissident was helped by one bloc and the others were helped by the other bloc, our countries were the losers and our citizens paid the price. Lives were lost, our economy became stagnant, we remained divided, fighting amongst ourselves up to nearly 60 years after the colonisation, and we still don't know what to do with our countries. We still don't know how to feed our citizens, how to train them.

We have no medicine labelled with our name on it for our people and our healthcare system has collapsed.

We are waiting for the west to come out with solutions for malaria, our own disease which doesn't even exist in the west. We are waiting for them to tell us how to produce crops. Sixty years after we said that we were able, we are still unable to show what we can do, we are still adopting the education system that has nothing to do with what we need, embracing techniques that have been abandoned for decades and using theories that are obsolete. What results and outcomes do we want?

I maintain that we are more than able and can do far beyond what we actually do. We are over one billion individuals and we represent a strong market. Our market potential is huge. We have the world's youngest population and still growing; this youth is dynamic and intelligent, we need to capitalise on this potential. We sing and chant that our youth is our future but we plan only for now, thereby giving no chance or opportunities to this future to release its potential. This should be our priority, to help them to make the most of their talents and open up opportunities for them to exercise and contribute. We should also give opportunities to our Diasporas that still identify themselves with us and facilitate their return and integration if they wish to do so. After all, who made the west rich? It was its Diasporas, explorers, merchants, imperialists, slave traders, and nowadays international corporations. These companies bring billions in taxes and millions of jobs to the country. In fact they are vital to the country and this explains why presidents, prime ministers, queens and kings negotiate trade deals for their countries. The state doesn't in reality produce anything, but they negotiate better deals for their countries' companies, which in turn bring billions into their economies.

Our diaspora is a huge force we can tap into. It has been estimated that African Americans have $1.1 trillion in buying power. Yet in the USA, they do not represent a clear visible group because of their lack of organisation and coherence. Lessons could be learned from this case in regard of our diaspora. However, we shouldn't rely only on our Diaspora because some, if not most, of them are loyal to neither us nor the west. They are in the middle, hesitating and understanding neither of the two systems. They want the west to act like the south and they want the south to have western systems. They are not happy anywhere. They complain here and there. Those of the Diaspora that could be useful are those who want to do something back home and have started to do it seriously. Sometimes, they see themselves as superior to those who have stayed home building on the culture of ego that we talked about at the beginning of this book, where we were told that some people were superior to others. They reject this theory officially because they fall into the inferior category when they are in the west, but embrace it officiously and individually when they are in the south because they want to exercise authority and dominance on others just because of the simple fact that they have travelled abroad.

They criticise that nothing has moved here, but in reality, they have not done anything to help the country or continent move forward. But there are many cases where our diaspora is defending, fighting and finding ways to help the continent. They have done many things, working with people in the continent to do so or advocating for the continent from where they are. They are our partners; we will discuss each partner's relationship in our power/interest spectrum.

We should learn from our past mistakes and correct

those we are making right now. In the past, we signed treaties with people to colonise us. We, from the continent, sent letters inviting people to come and colonise us even though the letters may have not expressly mentioned our need for colonisation; we nonetheless invited them to come to implement with us such systems they were establishing elsewhere. I am aware of one invitation from Cameroon in 1818 which reached Queen Victoria too late, when the French had already signed one, which became known as the "too late treaty". None of this turned out to be in our best interests, and from these treaties derived programmes that colonised our lands and our minds, thus reducing us to a bunch of servants and blessed, yes, yes.

We may have not authorised slavery or imperialism but we certainly – at least in some way – authorised colonisation and we continue to sign ridiculous contracts nowadays with China. We are signing off our resources, contracts and major projects to China which is now considered as the best partner of the day, forgetting that they are only interested in themselves, like others were in the past. When the battle becomes tense, they will sit on the table with the west to decide each other's interests and we will still be running after the best bidders as if we were unable to do anything by ourselves.

We can complain about other people stealing our resources but can we claim some sort of responsibility for this? Even if we have acted unconsciously due to a planned programming of our minds as I have argued throughout this book, we still need to recognise a part we played. I was told mirrors, salt and basic fabrics were given in exchange for our children, brothers and sisters that were taken as slaves, though many were taken by force. I am also told that contracts that were signed after the colonisation were worth peanuts. We signed them and without remorse, without due reflection and with a cool heart they took what they needed and continue to do so, whilst in our hearts, we naively believed in a true friendship amongst nations. This can only exist when the "rapport de force" is at least almost equal. Better contracts could have been signed just before the independences if we had been smart enough because they had no choice but to leave. At that time, we had an upper hand; we were in a better position for negotiations. We missed it. We didn't see far enough, because trained to be servants, we were acting as we were expected to.

Today, we continue to sign agreements that do not represent our interests, just because we are focused on the present. We had no long term plan then and we still don't have it now. We continue to sell, give, agree, and consent to all sorts of projects that will make us forever dependent and poorer. What a shame. We grow up criticising others and now that we are grown up and in charge, we are worse than our forefathers. Double tragedy! The fact is, we don't care about tomorrow, and we don't care about our future generations.

Can we believe that in 2005, China's export to Africa hit a new record high: US$14 billion? Products that are imported from China can easily be made in Africa. But instead of competing with them, we see them as an easy alternative.

It is evident that China's exports to Africa are machinery and electronics, textiles and apparel, hi-tech products and finished goods, while imports from Africa concentrate on crude oil, iron ore, cotton, diamonds and other natural resources and primary goods. What will happen if we refused to sell our crude oil and other products to China? They will not get them elsewhere cheaper. But are we getting the right price? Why don't we change the structure of the import and get them to build these industries here? Chinese companies have been reaping rich dividends by promoting their products and services in Africa, making our money bounce from our hands to their pockets.

A. Robinson (2001; 2002) has argued that Africa's relative poverty at the end of the 20th century was primarily the result of the form taken by European colonialism on the continent: Europeans settling for extraction, rather than settling themselves in overwhelming numbers and thereby introducing the kinds of institution (private property rights and systems of government that would support them) that, according to Acemoglu, Johnson and Robinson (2002), was responsible for economic development in Europe and the colonies of European settlement in North America and Australasia. The same mistake can be avoided today with China if we are vigilant.

Previous research also shows that colonial extraction in Africa could be seen most decisively in the appropriation of land for European settlers or plantations, a strategy used not only to provide European investors and settlers with cheap and secure control of land, but also to oblige Africans to sell their labour to European farmers, planters or mine-owners (Palmer and Parsons, 1977). There was coercive recruitment of labour by colonial administrations, whether to work for the state or for European private enterprise (Fall, 1993; Northrup, 1988). Today, we have the possibility to harness our efforts to bring about the change we want to see, whilst remaining vigilant in order to avoid oversight on contracts we sign with new partners like China. If our people were used to make the west rich, if our children were deported to build the USA, we can use the same method to build our land, using our people, who will at least this time work for their countries. We can create wealth together using our own people and our own resources. We can use our people to make our people rich. We can use what we have in the land to make our land richer. We can exploit our resources to improve what we have ourselves. We don't have to sell, sell, and sell. We can reserve what we can now if possible.

I watched a BBC documentary on Bakas of Cameroon, the Pygmies who were living their lives peacefully until a local introduced them to alcohol and since then, alcohol that was being sold to them made them become dependent to the point that they started losing their way of life. It just shows how lives can be ruined through progressive conditioning of people's minds. This is how we were also conditioned.

To regain our independence, we need to have projects, as many projects as we can think of, and put them in order of priority. These projects need to be what will help us create more resources or transform what we have, on one hand; and on the other hand, some of them need to be able to improve our infrastructures.

The money will come from our people and the work will be carried out by our people. This has been done everywhere in the developed countries. Russia was poor but by the time Lenin finished with his revolution, they had become an agricultural and industrial nation. The USA was almost an empty, uncultivated and nearly uninhabited land, but was built in less than 200 years and its building was done by our people who paid the price; but today the USA is the world's most powerful nation. This was the plan of its forefathers. We are the forefathers of the Africa of tomorrow. Let's plan now.

Most countries in Europe were built using people, with a lot of people losing their lives; the price was high at the time but the result is seen today and enjoyed by millions. Not that we don't die; we do, but with no results. If we use our people to build, some will die but this time for a good cause, a good reason. We will combine the use of our people with the use of machines that we will make ourselves. Whether we use our people to build Africa or not, we will lose people either through war that is due to no fault of ours, or through diseases, catastrophes etc. Life expectancy is under 50 in most African countries and people are dying of hunger, illness, hardship and so on. It is better we gather our people to create a better future for ourselves. To demonstrate that this has been done on a small scale and can be done more widely, I will pick a few examples before expanding other ways internal resources could be used to develop the country or target sectors with potential national or continental benefits.

In Cameroon, prior to the USA World Cup 1994, the country launched a fundraising campaign for the national team campaign. This campaign was called "Operation Coup de Coeur". It was a simple appeal to citizens to contribute whatever they had in order to secure the training of their national team. Encouraged by the performance of the team during the World Cup 1990 in Italy, people and companies across the country contributed around nine billion XAF. Of course this money never reached the players, but the momentum observed in that year and the ability to raise such a large sum of money for a national cause shows that more can be done by ourselves to raise our living standard. It also goes to show that money can be raised from our people if we associate them in projects and plans for our common good.

We do have money if we work with our people to secure the amount we require for any project. We just need good projects and proper leadership direction. As an illustration, the nine billion XAF could have been used to build 900 small manufacturers using 100 million XAF each, which could have employ a minimum of 2,700 citizens if each unit employed three people. If each of the companies created could generate revenue of 5% per annum, it would have generated 450,000,000 XAF each year. Imagine where we would have been by now. This is not a fiction, it is fact, and that could have been done. The truth is that between 1994 and 2014 there have been small companies that have been formed with less than 20 million XAF and that are now employing citizens, creating jobs and paying taxes. There are individuals that have gone from nothing to millionaires in this time as well. The benefit from such projects could have helped set up heavy machinery companies, started research centres in our chosen areas, etc. I am not going to suggest the setting up of cooperatives, because this becomes easily a structure managed from the top and members become observers.

In Burkina Faso, during Sankara's reign, cheap accommodations were built for citizens by citizens though a well organised system. In every city, bricklayers, carpenters, foremen etc. were identified, and every Saturday they came together to build houses. Where the state could, it provided zinc or cement and other construction materials, but most were provided by people themselves and bit by bit, 1200 accommodations were built (I lived there). In years two and three accommodations were built, and companies were set up. People were encouraged to use local produce and cloth produced locally. This became the object of national pride; a poor country was on its way up when this hope was quenched.

Sankara's development model has been called endogenous or self-centred development, which is a process of economic, social, cultural, scientific and political transformation, based on the mobilisation of internal social forces and resources and using the accumulated knowledge and experiences of the people of a country. Endogenous development allows citizens to be active agents in the transformation of their society instead of remaining spectators outside of a political system inspired by foreign models. In reality, endogenous development relies on its own strength. Professor Joseph Ki-Zerbo, who was one of the renowned historians in Africa and whom I had the privilege to meet and discuss this with him, said that, "It is by drawing from the elements of our own development that we develop ourselves." The concept that the Professor illustrates was inspired by Sankara. In fact, the Sankarist Revolution was one of the greatest attempts at popular and democratic emancipation in post-independence Africa. It has been considered by many, me included, as a novel experience of deep economic, social, cultural and political transformation as evidenced by mass mobilisations to get people to take responsibility for their own needs, with the construction of infrastructure such as dams, reservoirs, wells, roads and schools, social housing, through the use of the principle 'relying on one's own strength'.

For Sankara, true endogenous development was based upon a number of principles, among them:

- The necessity of relying on one's own strength
- Mass participation in politics with the goal of changing one's condition in life
- The emancipation of women and their inclusion in the process of development
- The use of the state as an instrument fro economic and social transformation

For Thomas Sankara, relying on one's own strength meant asking the people to think about their own development: most importantly, to give people confidence in themselves, the sense of self-belief without which one cannot be free, and to understand that ultimately we do all things if we want to and are resolute about doing them. This is my key message throughout this book. That our battle will start with self-belief; we need to win within before we can win without. We are stoppable only by limitations that we impose upon ourselves. The first Popular Development Plan (PPD), initiated by Sankara from October 1984 to December 1985, was adopted after a participatory and democratic process including the most remote villages. The financing of the plan was 100% Burkinabe. It must be noted that from 1985 to 1988, during Sankara's presidency, Burkina Faso did not receive any foreign 'aid' from the west, including France, nor the World Bank or the International Monetary Fund (IMF). He had relied entirely on his own strength and the solidarity of friendly countries sharing the same vision and ideals. Popular mobilisation, mainly through the Committees for the Defence of the Revolution (CDR), and the spirit of relying on one's own forces, saw 85% of the PPD's objectives realised. In one year, 250 reservoirs were built and 3000 wells drilled. This does not even take into account the other achievements in the fields of health, housing, education, agricultural production, etc. If this was done in a very poor country like Burkina Faso, it can be done anywhere in Africa. People may have their own opinions about the methods that were used, yet we have suffered worse. I lived in one of the houses built during Sankara's reign; it is now considered as a prime area of Ouagadougou. I lived in 265, 1200 Lodgements, a product of Sankara's revolution. I know similar initiatives can be undertaken here and there in Africa.

These examples are a testament that if we will, we can.

We can have first class manufactures; we can stop complaining about the effect of colonisation. After all, countries were also colonised in Europe; Belgium was in some ways colonised by France, India was colonised, Malaysia, Belgium, Switzerland etc. were somehow colonised. The Czech Republic was occupied, Germany was divided but this did not stop them from working, planning and striving in the midst of tribulations. Yes countries occupied by Germany have been compensated, and in the same vein I ask for Africa to be compensated by colonisers for their occupation, annexation and exploitation. Economic damages should be paid. Even though our resources are being used, exploited, our mind is still free to think, to dream, to imagine and to try new things that can set us free.

So, pending adequate compensation that will surely come, we need to continue to work toward a common vision of self-determination.

Australia was born not so long ago and is less populated than many of our countries, yet we desire to move there. These countries were not built by extraordinary people, no one has two heads and four legs in these countries; if they had, and it would be a surprise even to us. They are born of a mother and a father and have the same blood we have, they simply think independence, they simply refuse to see themselves as inferiors, they simply know that they can, they simply know that they are able to do anything as long as they put their mind to it.

In every domain, we blame others, even when our athletes can't perform, we blame the state. Yet success is a matter of personal sacrifice and endeavour. In Europe, athletes don't train for free. They pay for their training. Our players start here but when they are bought abroad, they become great world class players because they train even harder. For them to succeed locally, we need to plan and work on our plans. What our footballers have been able to do abroad, they can do back home if we are organised.

We should be planning for decades ahead, centuries to come; for sure, our needs will increase and our population will grow, these things are predictable. Based on forecasts, we can plan to build new roads, hospitals, homes, state buildings, cities, schools, public services. Like I said, our people are available and represent our assets. If we don't work with them, many will die of hunger, illness, malnutrition, hardships etc. If we act, some will complain of dictatorships and hard work, but in the end we will be better off together; it is better for some to die now to save tomorrow; we are dying anyway and no one is benefiting, but if we die of hard work, sowing towards the future, our works will remain and will be remembered. There will be for sure some imperfections in the system but along the way and with time, corrections will be made if we know exactly where we are going; we can readjust our speed and change the road if the shortcut is too dangerous to follow, and take the normal or long road. Provided we know where we are going, we will get there. Like I said, if we are resolute, we will be criticised even by our own people, but it all depends on who is judging.

When I was younger, the community used to come together every weekend to carry out works, whether digging new roads, cleaning or cutting the hedge. This made our roads better maintained and the state was not always involved. How many died as a result? Today in the name of modernity, such enterprises, such commitments are no longer observed. People do their things, rush after money, build their houses and pave their courtyard but find it difficult to get there. If this effort were made to improve the local area, we would all be better off. Henceforth, roads built by Germans and other colonising powers have had fewer additions to them. To the contrary, some of them have been abandoned. Railways and roads were built, without sophisticated engines, yet they were built with our people doing most of the works. People claim some died, it is true, but the roads remain and we have all benefited. We can replicate the same nowadays with the exception that few will die as a result because we have engines and better tools to carry out the work. We may not have enough money to pay huge salaries, but at least our people can work for free or we make the better-off contribute to the benefit of all. This should not only be done in the area of roads, but the country's overall infrastructure. We can farm fish, replenish our parks with animals; as we intensify our agriculture, we can intensify our meat and fish production. Aquaculture is an area we have not given much attention, yet we can all benefit from it. In our public services, we need to reduce rate tapes, overcome corruption. I note that each ministry in Africa has subdivisions all the way down to the departmental and local area. Those people are producing nothing but are paid by our government. Their budget can be used to develop manufacturing and other needed sectors in the country's economy.

Our administration system can be simplified and decentralised. We don't need each ministry to be represented everywhere, we just need a sound management system to speed and facilitate various tasks carried out by each sector. We may have one central office and with good communication facilities and postal system, we will get better results. This will mean fewer jobs in this sector, but the money saved will be used to create a vibrant economic system that will produce and employ even more people, who in turn will be better paid.

As it stands today, our greatest danger in public services is self-serving cronyism and the desire to bind citizens in endless, time-consuming red tape. Many of our people from the Diaspora, willing to do business back home, have confronted this harsh reality, and this explains why doing business across much of Africa is a nightmare. It has been estimated that in Cameroon, it takes a potential investor around 426 days to perform 15 procedures to gain a business licence, in Angola it takes 119 days filling out forms to start a business, whereas in the UK, you can incorporate your company in two hours, in the USA it can take up to 40 days and in South Korea 17 days. This goes to explain why it is easy to do business elsewhere than in Africa. I understand that this lengthy process has been reduced in Cameroon, but people still face the reality of corruption and carelessness from public service workers when it comes to delivering first class public services. We can improve this, we can change this, and we have the power to change this. The colonial power has no part to play here; at least now that we understand they designed this system to hinder us, we can get rid of it and implement what works for us. We can come out with a new model that will serve us better, we can start new projects that will benefit us and we know by now that money is not a problem. Our people are ready and await the first move from our leaders. Let's start, let's put our acts together, we are unstoppable unless we stop ourselves. The responsibility is in our hands, let's take it seriously. Each of us has a part to play and I am ready and await the call for duties.

Chapter 12:

What do we need and what do we have?

Wherever we find ourselves, there is always something that could help us move toward what we want. But the most difficult thing is to take the first step for our move. To take this first step requires faith. In the Bible, the widow of Zerephath was rewarded for her faith. She had oil jars which served as a channel for wealth to pay her debts. There is always something we have that can serve as a channel for our blessing, but to get what we want, we need to have a full understanding of our needs, current services and provisions and benchmark what we have against our present capabilities in order to understand the gap to bridge. Let's read the whole story of the widow of Zerephath: 1 Kings 17:7–24 New International Version (NIV):

Sometime later the brook dried up because there had been no rain in the land. Then the word of the LORD came to him: "Go at once to Zerephath in the region of Sidon and stay there. I have directed a widow there to supply you with food." So he went to Zarephath. When he came to the town gate, a widow was there gathering sticks. He called to her and asked, "Would you bring me a little water in a jar so I may have a drink?" As she was going to get it, he called, "And bring me, please, a piece of bread."

"As surely as the LORD your God lives," she replied, "I don't have any bread—only a handful of flour in a jar and a little olive oil in a jug. I am gathering a few sticks to take home and make a meal for myself and my son, that we may eat it—and die."

Elijah said to her "Don't be afraid. Go home and do as you have said. But first make a small loaf of bread for me from what you have and bring it to me, and then make something for yourself and your son. For this is what the LORD, the God of Israel, says: 'The jar of flour will not be used up and the jug of oil will not run dry until the day the LORD sends rain on the land.'"

She went away and did as Elijah had told her. So there was food every day for Elijah and for the woman and her family. For the jar of flour was not used up and the jug of oil did not run dry, in keeping with the word of the LORD spoken by Elijah.

Sometime later the son of the woman who owned the house became ill. He grew worse and worse, and finally stopped breathing. She said to Elijah, "What do you have against me, man of God? Did you come to remind me of my sin and kill my son?"

"Give me your son," Elijah replied. He took him from her arms, carried him to the upper room where he was staying, and laid him on his bed. Then he cried out to the LORD, "LORD my God, have you brought tragedy even on this widow I am staying with, by causing her son to die?" Then he stretched himself out on the boy three times and cried out to the LORD, "LORD my God, let this boy's life return to him!"

The LORD heard Elijah's cry, and the boy's life returned to him, and he lived.23 Elijah picked up the child and carried him down from the room into the house. He gave him to his mother and said, "Look, your son is alive!"

Then the woman said to Elijah, "Now I know that you are a man of God and that the word of the LORD from your mouth is the truth."

In addition to this story, I may add the story of Ismael's mother, who found a well just by where she was lying after she thought she would die of thirst. The two women knew exactly what they wanted and were able to express their need clearly, so that it had an adequate solution. If we are clear about what we want, and determined to get an answer, somehow, the solution will come even from an unexpected source. Like I said, solutions are never far from the problem.

But the problem is that to understand our need is a laborious task but it is necessary as it will give us a clear picture of what we need and what we currently don't have, as well as what we currently use that is not produced by us. This exercise will also help us to have a clear vision and a true picture of who we are, where we are and where we need to be. To do this we will need a good planning process as it will help us to identify critical paths, which will enable us to set up key milestones possible of spanning a period of 50 years and beyond. Of course governments will change, and each may have its priorities but if we have a clear road map as a nation, we will act in a way that all works together for our common good.

Most of the time, what we need is in conflict with what we have and we have to do with what we have in hand. We cannot keep substituting when we are able to get exactly our requirements; and we cannot keep buying from people when we have the ability to do things ourselves. Of course if our requirements are too costly they can be substituted or sourced elsewhere, but more often, we pay more than we should have paid because we can't be bothered to investigate the possibility of doing it ourselves. On many occasions, our needs are being dictated by other forces external to our nations such as: You need to privatise your public companies, you need to have new high speed internet connection, you need to join a new international network, you need to sign new treaties, and you need new programmes in your country. Remember that if we know exactly what we want, we will get it. What we want should be in line with what is useful to us. What we want should reflect the direction we are taking. In fact, what we want should be the reflection of what we need to use every day. When we start to do this, we will realise that we use what others make to the point that we have forgotten that our daily used products are imported. For example, what do we use every day:

- For cooking
- For building
- For bathing
- For driving
- For travelling
- For studying
- For teaching
- For clothing
- For sleeping
- For shaving
- For shipping
- For communicating
- For measuring
- For seeing
- For enjoying
- For protecting
- For reproducing
- For caring

This can then be broken down into various items; for example, for shaving we can divide into two: items for males and items for females; when we do this we will see that males need razor blades, clippers, aftershave etc. and we can identify which of these items we manufacture ourselves. Basically it appears that we make none of them! We see that the majority of items that we use in personal health are made by Unilever, such as Gillette razors, aftershave, cosmetics, etc.

For females there is a huge market. Hair Product, nail extensions etc. This is a huge market that we can tap into even though we have spoken our mind against excessive use of hair extensions as an alienating and unconscious act of self-rejection. This phenomenon will continue and we can step in and take over the market and start manufacturing some of these consumer goods ourselves, supporting this with marketing, mind transformation programmes and political programmes. Blocking importation of such products, or at least reducing their import, taxing heavily their import and subsidising our own where possible.

What do we use for travelling? This can include transport, travel equipment. Do we make travel bags internally? Can we make them? Do we manufacture cars, what will it take for us to do it? We have seen international collaborations. But we can train our own citizens to do it. Our taxis, we can find a way to make these; buses, other utility vehicles. Airlines, can we set up one if we have none etc.?

It doesn't matter if we only have a market of a couple of million units to sell, we can encourage a small group of experts in each area to set up small companies to manufacture and sell these things and we will begin to access regional markets, sub regional and international markets where possible.

For building, we can check from door hinges to roof materials and anything that we use in construction and find a way to manufacture most of them locally. This is a sector where we mostly import and what we produce locally cannot meet the demand; if this is the case, we will increase our capacity.

For dress, our textile companies will be revamped and capacities increased to meet national consumption and compete internationally. In each area, we could plan in the way that we know exactly how many people we need in each sector every year and train them accordingly. We can know exactly how many lawyers, how many nurses, how many mechanics we need.

It has been identified that Africa buys a lot of shoes and clothing as well as electrical goods from China and that almost 95% of such products are manufactured elsewhere and exported to Africa. We can easily make most of them if we want to. We sell cotton that is used to make cloth that they resell to us at a more expensive price. Most of our clothing is imported; if we don't import the ready-made, we will buy the fabrics. We sell petroleum products and they are used to manufacture clothing, medical equipment and cosmetics that are sold back to us ten times more expensively etc.

The centre for African studies in the US Department of Education did research on imports and exports in Africa and it appears that almost all African countries export the same commodities to similar buyers, and that we spend more on import than we export for. Furthermore, sub-regional trade was very low or limited. This means that few African countries trade amongst themselves. They also argued that most African economies remain largely agrarian, dependent on agriculture and other natural resources as the major source of foreign exchange and employment. However, many African countries are striving to diversify their income base, creating numerous opportunities for trade and investment by interested foreign partners. Currently, major exports are agricultural commodities and minerals and import demand centres on manufactured products. If we were truly agrarians, we wouldn't so be hungry. The little we produce is sold elsewhere whilst our people are starving, thereby creating internal inflation. This inflation can only be controlled by an agricultural revolution and limitation of the export. We need to review our needs and put more effort into producing what we need. There are no industries and no sectors we cannot enter if we are willing to. We have brains that are not being used. With new technologies and the internet today, it has become even easier to learn what we don't know by a simple click.

Part Three:

A New Dawn

Chapter 13:

My political programme

I have already said that we can do all things that we plan to do if we want to. If other countries have succeeded, we can also achieve our desired plans for our people. I have a plan, I have a programme and I will go from a belief that impossibility is the limitation we impose upon ourselves. From my own perspective, nothing is impossible to he who believes. But achieving great things starts with small things that people often take for granted. We watch TV, but we have not tried to make one. We think, as a country, that making them is someone else's responsibility. If we need these things, why not investigate the possibility of making them ourselves? To highlight the point we are a nation or continent of consumers rather, I will tell you the story of a simple toothpaste that we are unable to make, or toothbrush, of which we cannot produce any. Yes, almost none.

I was preparing for my trip back home. I bought toothbrushes and toothpastes; as I was doing so; my wife was not in agreement with me because she was of the view that I was overloading myself whilst these things could be bought in Africa at an even cheaper price. Despite her insistence, I carried on and bought everything I needed and promised to give them to someone if we didn't need them. Even so, she was still adamant that there were not worthy as gifts. I insisted, "let us take them; we can always give them to someone in the village". At least they will gladly use I packed toothbrushes and toothpaste in the suitcase. Once we arrived, on the first day, most of them had disappeared, and people continued to take them, begging like they were luxurious products. The next day, we had none left including the toothpaste we had begun using; they had been taken away by family members who were desperately in need. I went to the shop to buy new toothbrushes and paste. I couldn't find any good toothbrushes, even the cheapest in Africa were five times more expensive than the average quality we've bought in Europe. Hence, we were not sure where they had been manufactured, and they visibly presented health risks. My wife was with me and was amazed how common items like toothbrushes could be so expensive and inaccessible to average people. I had just proved my point. This was because most products sold back home were imported. Razor blades, needles, sewing rods, lamps, clothing buttons, combs, hair products, perfumes, spaghetti, flour, rice, even beer, meat and fish were being imported due to lack of local supply.

There were few or no manufacturers in place for products of first consumption. Basic products that we use every day and take for granted after my assessment were all imported. Products and items that have been around for a long time and which have become a necessity for each individual. It was surprising that no one bothered to set up factories to produce them. No one questioned their origin and where they were produced and some assumed that they were produced locally, due to their nature and their local demand. This observation confirmed my suspicion that we produced nothing, and that almost 90%

of our everyday household products were manufactured elsewhere. In fact, we lived on imported products and have not tried to bring about substitutes or produce them ourselves. Our reliance on foreign imports cripples our economy and makes our lives extremely expensive. The biggest losers were the poor, children and older people. Only a minority of the population could afford products of necessity. I understood why we had such a high level of corruption, crimes and fake products. Imitation has developed tremendously, but products are not imitated in an acceptable way. People will take a particular cosmetic product's bottle and pour in anything that they can mix with the original product, such as perfume, just for it to smell alike. This fake product will be sold at a fraction of the product's cost. People who buy it become therefore exposed to serious health risks.

I know for sure that the African market is price sensitive. People want good or fairly good quality products at a reasonable price. In some cases, they just want to have an item, such as a TV set, car, etc. They know that these items could be repaired if they break down. So the entry price is an incentive for them. If they can acquire an item at a relatively low price and easily have access to cheap and easily accessible replacement parts, they will buy it. This is why in recent years, Chinese goods have emerged as popular items of trade among African countries and Chinese companies are exporting in increasing quantities a wide variety of products directly to the African markets. As a result, China's trade with Africa has been registering a substantial growth in recent years.

Our people know that Chinese goods are not of high quality, but at least they can afford them. What we are observing and tolerating of China today will in time be considered as a form of colonisation and dominance.

Imperialism started the same way, with treaties, agreements, joint working and so called friendships. When we know that only interests exist between nations, it will be pure blindness to assume that China will be our friend. They are craving the natural resources which we have, they are giving us what we assess as cheap loans but which in reality are nothing compared with what they are reaping. They are even importing their population to fill our land and when there are contracts financed by Chinese, they send their people to work on these projects. They do wholesale and retail at the same time thereby cutting out local people who buy wholesale from them and are unable to break even; they become bankrupt and leave the market, which is then captured by the Chinese.

We should aim at setting up our own manufacturing to produce the same goods we buy elsewhere or ensure that those who sell those products in our countries set up manufacturing there to produce them. We shouldn't be about to settle for alternatives or dependency on other people. We should strive to know and understand our true worth and generate internal means to bring it to light. We should be able to understand what we have, and find the best way to put this into use. Once we start transforming our resources, when we start to depend much on what we have and make it valuable, people will start to negotiate with us on equal terms. We should know our bottom line when bargaining or negotiating with other nations. But if we have petrol and are unable to exploit it, have no plan to exploit it ourselves but yet want to exploit it, our partners will always buy it cheaply unless we know our bottom line.

The USA has the highest petrol reserve in the world, they are not in a hurry to exploit them, but for us, as soon as we are told that we have natural resources somewhere, we rush into unworthy contracts to exploit them during our term in power. We don't care what price we get and we don't care if we are being fooled. For us, the most important thing is to have what we can have now. We don't in turn use the income to manufacture what could be useful to our citizens and as a result, we end up paying over the odds for transformed products from our land.

Knowing that our market is price sensitive, we should be able to find solutions to cater for our people who have welcomed the easy availability of low-priced Chinese goods. Our traders and merchants have also been quick to seize the opportunity to source their requirements from China in order to increase their profit margins, yet if they had these opportunities at home, they would embrace them.

Business people are more concerned with profit margin and client base. If they could have a good client base for products which sell with a good profit margin, without the need to go far from home, they would buy them. As we can see, China is now considered as a new world and we are all singing their songs all over Africa. Remember we sang the same songs at the beginning of the colonisation. We act as if we had no choice in Africa, even if we were better informed. Almost all African countries have been flooded with low-priced Chinese goods. Whether it is tyres, automobile parts, stationery, perfumes, cosmetics, computer hardware, furniture or machinery, China has dominated the African markets. Can we make these things? I would say yes, we can make most of them. Are we going to make them? Most people will say no. Why? People will point to the state and infrastructures. Yet most developed nations have benefited from individual initiatives. Our people will need endorsement. And our trade deals should stop focusing on our resources that people are invited to use and then exploit at will.

My needs inventory I earlier discussed will be geared toward assessing citizens' needs, carrying out an inventory of what is used in households on a daily basis and finding a better way to manufacture it in the country. My inventory will go from needles to more sophisticated tools and will also cover food and items used in the house such as soap, machines, cutlery etc. The understanding gained from the population's needs assessment will be used to help make decisions about how to prioritise the allocation of our resources to meet the needs that have been identified, alongside other ways in which people's needs are met.

We already have a demographic profile of our populations and this will help us understand the level of needs. With our needs assessment we will be able to identify current and projected future population sizes; the current and future composition of the population by age, gender, geographic location, urban–rural location, household composition including marital status and specific population subgroups, such as ethnic groups.

This needs to be combined with information about the effectiveness and cost-effectiveness of available interventions. Decisions about priorities will need to reflect local priorities and circumstances and to be informed by available resources and what is feasible in practice. We need to start this programme with full stomachs. We need a proper agricultural revolution. We cannot work in total serenity if we are hungry. We have land, rich soil, we have trained countless numbers of engineers in agriculture and agricultural techniques are readily available. We know how to do serious agriculture; we just want this to become one of our core priorities.

Chapter 14:

We need to feed out people

Agriculture is an important factor in economic development. Although this fact is known and has been highly promoted by various African leaders, not much has come out of it. Most African independences were followed by a boom in agriculture, but local populations were fooled by promoters as they focused only on export products such as cacao and coffee. If the effort put into developing coffee and cacao farms were dedicated to food growth, famine would have disappeared in Africa. In 2012, three U.N. agencies said nearly 239 million in Africa were hungry, a figure that was about 20 million higher than in 2008. This is a controversy when we know that Africa has around 600 million hectares of uncultivated arable land, roughly 60 percent of the global total, According to an influential recent analysis, published by McKinley.

History tells us that every developed nation started by developing agriculture. A nation cannot be developed if its citizens are going hungry and much cannot be done if what is nationally produced cannot feed 30% of the population. When one is hungry, one cannot do much. Hunger and malnutrition are the cause of some deaths and low life expectancy in many Africans, due to hardship and lack of people's ability to meet their basic needs. Most of the time, about 80% depend on subsistence agriculture but what is grown is not enough to meet their personal needs, yet they have to sell some of their produce to buy other products of necessity such as soap, salt, cooking oil etc., which we now know are mostly imported.

Proper agriculture, otherwise known as intensive agriculture, will help the nation to breathe. People will have enough to meet their personal needs. If there is enough production, the price will fall and costs of other essential products reduce. The consumer price index is commonly used to determine the level of inflation in most developed countries, but in Africa, prices are very unstable and inflation extremely high due of our over dependence on imports, lack of local ability to cater for our needs and the fragility of our infrastructures, and most importantly our agriculture. We depend on the mercy of the rain even though water abounds in Africa that can be used to irrigate land. It has been assessed that 80 percent of Africa's agriculture still depends on rain not irrigation. We understand why African cereal yields for example are just over one-third of the developing world average and have barely increased in 30 years.

It is commonly accepted that agriculture is the source of livelihood for more than half of the world's population. In some countries more than four-fifths of the inhabitants support themselves by farming, while in the more industrialised countries the proportion range is much lower but the quantity of food produced is often enough to meet the population's needs. It is not so much about how many people are considered as farmers, it is how much is produced from our farms. Is the production enough to meet local need? We don't want 90% of people to be farmers, but we want those who are skilled farmers to dedicate their time to doing what they have the passion to do.

When I was younger, we had farms, I worked in our farms most of the time and I didn't like it. This was not my passion. In fact neither my dad nor mum were keen farmers. They did it because they needed to survive and paying our school fees depended on the farm revenues. In general, when a large fraction of a nation's population depends on agriculture for its livelihood, average incomes are low. This is why most people living in our villages have very low income, because they solely depend on their farming revenues. This goes with Jamsetji Tata, the founder of one of the wealthiest companies in the world, who suggested that, "what advances a nation or a community is not so much to prop up its weakest and most helpless members, but to lift up the best and the most gifted, so as to make them of the greatest service to the country. Business is sustainable only when it serves a larger purpose in society". "In a free enterprise the community is not just another stakeholder to business, but is in fact the very purpose of its existence." So we will need to identify our best farming areas, our gifted farmers and help them to become the best in the area of agriculture in order to bring production up, which will be advantageous to all.

I can say with certitude that our nations are poorer because most of our population is engaged in agriculture, lives on it and depends on it, despite not knowing how to do it well. If everyone producing was able to sell, we would still be poor because other areas of our economy would be less developed. We need a developed sector of agriculture that will produce enough to cater for people's needs; this can be done by 5% of the population if this is well done and supported by a visionary political initiative. A new government should focus on identifying areas of potential in the agriculture and apply the right strategy to develop it. There are products that can strive over others in each part of the country, this is traditionally known, but there are crops that need trying and developing. We have to have engineers in agriculture; if we don't have those who are able to assist, we will train them if we are willing.

In looking back upon the history of the more developed countries, I can say that agriculture has played an important part in the process of their enrichment. For one thing, if development is to occur, agriculture must be able to produce a surplus of food to maintain the growing non-agricultural labour force. Since food is more essential for life than are the services provided by merchants or bankers or factories, an economy cannot shift to such activities unless food is available for barter or sale in sufficient quantities to support those engaged in them.

Unless food can be obtained through international trade, a country does not normally develop industrially until its farm areas can supply its towns with food in exchange for the products of their factories, this is a fact and I hold it as a truth for now. We know for sure that we have been obtaining food from international trade and this is why we can't have enough, and more, why our citizens are going hungry. We should therefore focus on developing this sector to the point that surplus becomes the norm. In Europe, they were paying farmers not to produce too much milk and farmers are still subsidised. People may lack everything in Europe, but not food, and this is why corruption is limited. People will not sell their soul to eat, because there is enough around to eat.

Vice like corruption, crimes, insecurity and theft have something to do with deprivation, and people are corrupt because they want to amass for tomorrow. They are not sure they will hold any position tomorrow and once appointed, they see it as an opportunity to secure a future for themselves and their children. But if they were sure that they could easily find a job, if they were to leave their present job, and if they were able to meet their basic needs, they would think twice before selling public services to make money for themselves. They would think a bit before washing stamps for resale, they would think twice before asking for a bribe before tax or a bill can be paid. They would deliver the service they have been contracted to do, this would attract more money for the structure, and in turn, they would have a wage increase. If people had enough to eat, they would not sell themselves for a cheap buck.

A good government, our government of choice, will therefore encourage the production of agriculture that will not only produce a surplus of food for towns, but also produce the increased amount of food with a relatively smaller labour force. We will do our best to substitute human power by introducing labour-saving machinery. Agriculture will also be a source of the capital needed for industrial development to the extent that it provides a surplus that may be converted into the funds needed to purchase industrial equipment, or to build roads and provide public services. This justifies our focus on agriculture as a priority for our country of tomorrow.

The Guardian, an English newspaper, published an article on 8/06/2013 on eight ways to solve world hunger. The article suggested that Europe became wealthy and to a certain degree developed by going from hand production methods to machines, new chemical manufacturing, new ways of producing, and farming brought about steady changes in people's lives, making it easier to produce, reducing hard labour and improving people's living conditions. It further suggests that by adopting new ways of producing and working, almost every aspect of daily life was influenced including average income, which caused the population to exhibit unprecedented sustained growth, thus, a sustained standard of living for the general population followed. We can see that before the industrial revolution in Europe and USA, the majority of Americans lived on farmland, small towns, or villages where there was little manufacturing. A farmer was also able to make shoes, and the women spent their days making soap or making clothing as is the case in Africa. But people lived in fear that the crops they grew might fail, as many of them already suffered from malnutrition. In addition, diseases and other epidemics were unfortunately common as is still the case in our countries. To overcome these barriers and ensure food security, they moved to intensive agriculture and this lifted them above the crowd until they became the world power. This should be our next focus. To produce enough for our people; this can be done without delay and should be our first priority and because intensive agricultures requires the use of machines, our plan is revolutionary in the area of industries. This will also require the reorganisation of our systems.

Chapter 15:

Industrialising the continent and reorganising our systems

We want to create manufacturing companies where everyone can work as a partner but gets paid. I have already discussed how people came together in Cameroon and in Burkina Faso to either gather a tremendous sum of money that could have created 900 small companies or, in the case of Burkina Faso, how citizens came together to create infrastructures that would have required billions of XAF to develop. This was done using citizens themselves. Similar systems could be developed and help us overcome our limitations and challenge our self-imposed mental limitations that make us believe that we are poor.

Some people will call this Value Creation and Corporate Citizenship, but we will not go down the route of cooperatives. Starting with our needs assessment, we will identify what we need and use regularly that we don't produce and start setting up manufacturers, from the easiest to start with, to the most difficult. This will be done for our people, by our people, using our people and mobilising our internal resources.

The Cameroon's model of "Coup de Coeur" will be an easy way to start with, but more time and power will be invested in training, motivating and raising local leadership to take the destinies in hand. Resources are available and will be found where needed. Talents are available and will volunteer to work for mutual benefits. I know how wilful our populations are. Their problem is the lack of the central government input and drive. This will be put in place and support will be provided.

We have already indicated how mind transforming programmes will take place, starting with the restructuring and redesigning of our education programme which will create specialised citizens with able heads, not full heads. Amongst these citizens we will have builders, product designers, concept engineers, machine builders, structural and architectural engineers who will oversee our major projects and programmes. This is possible. We are moving a step closer. Through our common endeavour, we will fill the void where necessary, capitalise on new ideas. The funding for each venture will come from our citizens, who will be the owners; we will ensure our banks support us along the way as they will be reorganised to suit our local needs and culture.

Reorganisation of the banking system

Our economy will become vibrant if we can open up the market to investors, but measures will be put in place to ensure that external corporate businesses don't buy out everything we have. Conditions will be drawn at the right time, but our banking system will change from simply being a depository of people's money to a vibrant banking system where money can produce more, and citizens can access credit and investment, which in turn will create interest and generate surplus. Many people simply keep their money at home in Africa; there are reasons why they do so. We can find a better way to help keep this money as close to home as possible. We will help them keep their money where they can see it and use it any time they wish. We will transform traditional ways of moving money around whilst ensuring that people have access to credit and micro finance. Our change in the land ownership and cadastral system will support our banking system in reviewing their secured loan policies.

Setting up regulatory bodies and make prices transparent

Regulatory and professional bodies will be set up in various sectors to regulate their activities, with the primary aim of protecting the public. Unlike professional bodies, they will be established on the basis of legal mandate and set standards for each sector. Regulatory bodies will exercise a regulatory function, that is: imposing requirements, restrictions and conditions, setting standards in relation to any activity, and securing compliance, or enforcement. They will cover a wide variety of professions, to protect, promote and maintain health and safety, healthy competition, prevent abuses of the public by ensuring proper standards in the practice. Some of these agencies exists but are not strong enough, and since the deregulations, African prices have become very volatile and not transparent at all. The same item bought elsewhere for 1000 XAF can be purchase at double or triple the price somewhere else. Our people should not feel that they are being ripped off; they should have confidence in what they buy and have some sort of guarantee for products' purchase. We will tackle this area with fairness and our insurance reform will support this programme.

Encourage sub regional trades, simplify the company and land registry system

I briefly discussed how trade amongst African states was very limited. Diplomatic efforts and African integration that I have also discussed at the beginning of this book will offer a space for such initiative. Intensive diplomatic efforts and sub-regional structures will be used to make this possible. Strong leadership is required for better integration at the regional and sub-regional level. Roads could be built to link practically all African countries by land and railways will follow. Better integration also means free movement of people and goods.

Africa has just over one billion people. This is a huge market and amongst ourselves we can trade and prosper. A well-integrated and coordinated integration means that goods will freely move from one corner to the other and where necessary, wastes will be eliminated through a simple process of shipping goods from where they abound to where they are needed and so forth.

Our people need to be free to move and work where they want within Africa. This will not prevent any nation of becoming richer and if needs are properly identified; major hubs will be built and consolidated according to identified potential, balanced against possible outcomes in terms of revenues.

Africans need to work together, despite our differences in terms of cultures, there are more similarities and we face the same future. It is better to work together to secure the best for our future generations. Regional and sub-regional organisations need to be reinforced and given more power to act in our common interest, but we need to avoid the sell-out of these organisations; in simple terms, we should fund these organisations ourselves rather than getting the west to finance them; this will help us maintain our independence and follow our own vision. We should, as much as possible, find better ways to fund our projects. There is money in Africa to do this, we just need a political will and leadership determination; but where funding is a problem, our people will intervene as we associate them to the vision.

We will make it easier to set up companies by simplifying the process of registering a company and will make public contracts more open, fair and transparent. A social values act could be introduced where necessary to facilitate access to staring-up companies and a clear check and balance will be implemented to ensure clearer governance of public contracts.

The land registry reform

The land registry system is somehow chaotic apart from a few countries like Burkina Faso where the state has a clear and simplified system. We will also ensure a reorganisation of the land system and set up a new electronic land registry system to facilitate ownership, access to credit, loans and solve cadastral problems. As it stands, the state must protect the integrity of its territory. This means that the state must protect its land; to protect the land; it must first know and account for every inch of the whole land. This work will be done with the community and land owners. The most important step will be to know who owns what and where, and record it. So every piece of land will be recorded and each owner will be recorded; everywhere there will be automatic release or relinquishing of some land to the state for future development. Local people will decide where future admin buildings will be; this will also be recorded. The registers of lands will be computerised and certificates issued to owners against a fee; however, the fee will be proportional to the value of land, location and usage types. But all lands will be subject to stamp duty and annual tax levy, even if they represent a copper penny. This will help to check that owners are still claiming ownerships and when this stops, the state will take the land if there isn't someone to redeem it. In some cases, land could be sold by the state where necessary. All land and their owners will be in the public domain, accessible against a small fee, and land transactions will be regulated and processes put in place to record the sales or transfer of land and properties in an easy, quick and effective way.

Our reorganisation of the land registry will reflect the modern world in which we are today. This has been done in Europe; for example in the middle of the 19th century, many countries in Europe had problems with their land registry. Lands and real estate properties were doubly registered and the land and real estate cadastre was created for the purposes of the state and politics for taxation, negation and mortgaged real estate.

The land registers were aiming at security of ownership, the assuredness of land transactions, as well as the creditors' interests. This ensured that land was not registered twice but, most importantly, for African countries, the reorganisation and the land registry system means that people cannot sell the same land twice and that ownership can be verified without complications.

This system will be useful to the public, the state and the banks. The land registry reform will have a very strong need for developing the information technology and computerisation of cadastre and land registry system. The land registry reform will be an effective tool to avoid land disputes but also, we will have a single authority organisation to manage the registry and to make it easier for the public, as there will be a single point for decision making. It will finally help land owners to use their lands as secured collateral, to borrow for investment. Considering that the poorer people are land owners in Africa, this change will bring major improvement in their living condition.

Designing of new towns, cities, postal coding system, roads, and access to water and electricity

Our cities are not properly planned and we build anyhow. Very often, people face demolition and we don't have any sewer systems, which makes it very difficult to manage waste. This is part of our programme, that new centres and any new residential zone will have proper planning so as to include water, sewers, waste management, electricity etc. Each town will be meticulously planned and each city and village will have a plan for future growth, with agricultural lands, industrial land as to include future expansion plans. Our plans will also include incentives for private and public initiatives, for example new roads will be built or sold to private investors who could build and manage them for a set number of years, allowing them to recoup their investment. Railways, urban transport including tramways and underground lines will be encouraged, with private and public entities coming together to build these infrastructure for share gaining.

Reorganisation of birth, marriage and death register

Conditions for obtaining citizenship will be reorganised so as to prevent people from registering here and there, and ensuring that proper filiations are verifiable. This will also facilitate the re-issuing of lost birth or marriage certificates. Any citizen who loses such will pay a small admin fee for their certificate to be reprinted and there will be no need for certificates of citizenships for administrative forms like it is the case in many African countries today. A single document like passport will be enough to proof who one is. In this context, National Identity card could be done quicker as well as passports, and there will be a system in place to verify citizens and confirm their identity and filiation where necessary.

Car registration will be centralised and the role of the police will be focused on ensuring citizens' security, including crime prevention, rather than stopping people at will and asking for their ID or taking bribes. All administrative services will have Closed Circuit TV cameras fitted to deter fraud and corruption and counter fraud and corruption agencies will be set up. We will not neglect any sector. Additionally we will ensure the reorganisation of the army, the reorganisation of the country's intelligence system, media, and the reorganisation of the school system and training programmes. If for any reason, CCTVs are not fitted, we will have serious check and balance and reporting procedures whereby, each public sector worker reports for their action and contracts will be fair while ensuring that corrupt citizens are removed from public duties. As we work with our people and reorganise ourselves internally, we will also need to review the way in which we manage our external relations, starting with a change in our relationship spectrum.

Chapter 16:

Changing our relationship spectrum

How we are viewed by the world is important, but how we project ourselves to the world is even more important. Clearly, we can't move an inch, nor can we go far if we walk in complete ignorance of what goes on around the world.

We need to understand the forces that rule the world and we need to understand various networks that are working for or against us, though some do not declare themselves working against us, we need to understand how they work in order to adjust our strategies. Each network and each block is simply doing what they need to do to protect their interest and as such, they are always a step ahead.

I have to be straight here that I am not coming against anyone or attacking any groups. I am presenting how clever people organise themselves in order for us to rethink, reshape our behaviour and review our strategies. It is an alert to show how people can organise to defend their interests.

In Africa, we are mostly interested in the present and African companies have not tried to go international, nor do they attend meetings that change the world. How many Think Thanks do we have and how powerful are they? How much do we study about other countries' plans concerning us? Have we opened our eyes to see what has been hidden and what has been done in the closet in order to anticipate on moves and strategies of other strategies of other countries that have a potential of hindering our policies or our interests? Successful Nations strategise, organise and plan ahead. They are proactive, not reactive. Do we have the likes of Chatham House?

Chatham House has a profile of each African Country and can suggest an entry strategy to every European or North American company planning a move to Africa. African politic is discussed during Chatham House's meetings. Their findings are made available and can be used by powerful companies or people who want to do things in Africa and they clearly say that their participants are free to use the information received, but neither the identity nor the affiliation of the speaker(s) nor of any other participant may be revealed. The Bilderberg Group adopt the same rules. This is just for us to know that every one of our moves is studied and known in advance, our behaviours, our land; our people are studied by our competitors who know exactly which strategies should be used against us, and how to penetrate each African country. If we want to do better for ourselves, we equally need to study our partners alike, with seriousness and dedication. This means spending on research and information. Just look how many companies support Chatham House and see how prosperous those companies are. Just check how many governments are members of the Bilderberg Group and see how stable and rich they are. Just look at people who attend the Bilderberg Group meetings and check how influential they are and so forth.

If we want to be free, if we want to be stable, we have to align ourselves in such a way that people don't see us as a threat. But equally, we need to be quick to think and have our own networks of influence, power and control. I believe that we can have a new relationship spectrum with the world. For example we may not know much about them; most people will argue that Bilderberg Group is a secretive body attempting to shape the direction of the world and they take a step forward to preserve the interests of their respective countries in Europe and North America. This is a clear picture of how the world really works. We know that we do not wrestle against flesh and blood, but against principalities, against powers, against the rulers of the darkness of this age, against spiritual hosts of wickedness in the heavenly places (Ephesians 6:12, New King James Version (NKJV)). The battle field is somewhere else and only through careful planning and strategic moves can we balance the game. We are now perfectly aware of what is going on. We know that each programme, each act and movement toward Africa is not innocent and benevolent. We know that we are being watched and studied and that remaining so will only comply with what is regarded by others as the normal and expected outcome. But we can change the game to our advantage and others will not necessarily lose, and in my view, no one will lose. We can all be better off together, we can all be rich together and the wealth can increase in the world. Africans don't have to be at the bottom for the rest of the world to prosper; we can be amongst the frontrunners but it is up to us to negotiate this. We know our stakeholders and their relative power and interest. If we do not, we need to.

For now, we behave like poor people, a poor continent; yet literature and research paint our richness and diversity. Our position in the world map, our wealth, and our weather should have been a source of pride, but instead of using this to our advantage, we go around playing the victim in order to beg for hand-outs that have never and will never solve our problems. This doesn't help us and scares some people who have never been in contact with Africans and who have never been curious enough to learn about Africa. This lack of awareness and culture, added to the misery we project to the outside world, has intensified prejudice and stereotypes against Africans. Racism exists and we are the first targets. This situation can be reversed and it will be reversed when we transfer the change process from physical to psychological arena. We know that our fight is a spiritual battle and we will prepare a strong psychological warfare to take our rightful place.

Physically we will never win. We have no sophisticated weapons, no access to sophisticated arsenals and we have signed an agreement never to pursue or undertake to make atomic weapons. In fact, we sign everything without thinking, thus falling into traps set against us. We signed for the International Criminal Court of Justice, which has become a central stage to judge and condemn us, including our presidents who are still in power. This court has become an imperial court. I am not supporting any crimes committed against humanity, but I am saying that I have not seen any prime minster or head of state elsewhere pursued when they are still in power.

This court should change its focus to step in only when the country itself refuses to act and when perpetrators are difficult to capture by the country in which their crimes were committed. Furthermore, presidents, if they are to be judged, should be judged when they step down or when they are removed from power. What I see is that we are being dragged to court when we are still serving. This scenario is the same used during the imperialism whereby our kings were deposed, judged, condemned and killed in front of their people for crimes that they did not commit.

Today, we see that our presidents are the only ones who are judged in The Hague. If Gaddafi had not been assassinated, he would have been brought there to be judged; he was killed along with members of his family, the country lost thousands of souls and they are still losing citizens, but this has not been reported as a crime against humanity. I am sure perpetrators will not be judged, at least when it favours some people.

I am saying that if we want to remove dictators, let us not kill more people than they did. For example, we have situations where an attempt to remove dictators has created more instability that before and reduced citizens' ability to strive. If it becomes necessary to force a so called dictator from power, let us not commit more atrocities than they would have committed, and let us have a plan for peace after them; otherwise we fall into chaos and end up worse. While Iraq is going all pear shape, no one has been brought to justice over atrocities committed in the attempt to remove Saddam from power.

We understand that Saddam killed thousands of people, not that we accept what he did, but we say that there was a way to resolve the issue, not to add more damage to what had already been done. No one is safe in Iraq more than 10 years after Saddam was killed, but who takes responsibility? Will those who committed this crime ever be brought to account for their crimes? I am not the one to answer; I am just looking at how the balance of power works. In this context, can we really risk any physical confrontation? No, the result is predicted long before we start. But we can win, if we tap into the unseen world where everything is conceived before manifestation. This needs to start in our own mind, we need to believe that we are truly free and can do what we want, without risking any physical fight with anyone. Once we have the real strategies, which will come without fail, we can engage in what people will call diplomacy, tactics of words, ideological positioning.

Our positioning will start with our understanding of our key stakeholders. This means understanding who we are really dealing with, not guessing who they are. We will understand them when we know exactly how they operate as to identify their weaknesses. Everyone, everything has a weakest point; we just need to take our time to look for it. When we know this, we will devise the right strategies to work with them.

The key difference between diplomatically clever countries and those who are not, the key difference between nations that build good relationships externally and those who do not, resides in their ability to build links with key partners and stakeholders, with a clear understanding of each stakeholder's strengths and weaknesses. These links begin within the public sector including those who manage key sectors of the national economy, and who in turn will be trained to identify and manage the broader range of constituent stakeholder groups within their scope of activities.

The significance of identifying and managing stakeholder relations in government and government projects must become a priority. Key players in our public services should and will be trained to understand how such relationships can be strategically managed.

This will include our ability to deal with managerial behaviour in response to so-called partners or international corporations. Whether it relates to our natural resources or competition for key services provisions that yield profit, there will be numerous parties involved, directly or indirectly. Their needs and requirements must be identified and properly managed to bring us maximum benefits and stability.

Our questions will be: who is interested in what concerns us? Who is interested in which resources or services? What power do they have? Who has power that we can use to our benefit, even if they are not interested in us; what will it take for us to get them interested and at what price? Will the price be worth it? Who shall we keep as key partners and how do we get rid of those who benefit us not, but who hold positions of power? Who amongst our partners can help us overcome the threat posed by our foes? Who shall we keep as key partner and for what? Who should be ignored completely? Obviously, this may be a country that we have been working with in the past that is not adding any value to us and has no prospect of doing so, but their position of power should also be minimal. Yes we might be trading with them, that is all, but we don't just want trade; we want added value. People who will stand up for us, defend our cause, not just because they have something to lose, but because together we will lose and these countries must have international credibility. With these countries, we should forge a close alliance through negotiation and balance, ensuring that we come out as equal partners.

Mapping our key partners and stakeholders

I am using the stakeholder mapping power/interest matrix adapted from Mendelow (1981), who presented a model of environmental scanning in the context of the stakeholder concept, which includes the dynamism of the environment and the power of the stakeholder. Mendelow suggested that power and dynamism are relevant factors; low to high and static to dynamic. In my view, our moving forward will include our understanding of each stakeholder's interests and negotiating both individually and collectively where necessary. European countries had agreed never to go to war against each other again. Despite their disagreements, they don't fight each other because they know the price they would pay. We can do this amongst ourselves and with the west. In fact, this agreement between us and the west is necessary so no one will hide behind a no flight zone to destroy and destabilise our nations.

Our grasp of the nature of the relationships between various countries and their interactions with Africa includes culture and power relationships, and managing relationships with our key partners can result in much more than just their exploitation of whichever resources they want; it might become necessary to bring about intangible, socially complex issues that may enhance our ability to supplant or defeat our foes and secure long-term stability and progress for our people. It is clear that where there has been no war, there has been more prosperity and security for investors. We may, at some point, manage our tongue, let's say, avoiding direct provocations which have not helped in the past apart from costing the lives of those who spoke so loudly, and after they were gone we returned to the same situation.

If resources are being exploited, when we cannot do it ourselves, and we have no track record of doing so, we should then after understanding our needs and gaps work as I proposed above to create local or national structures that will progressively close the gaps, imitating where necessary to the point that our needs become locally met. If we do so, we will reach a point where our imports and exports are balanced and we will have locally developed industries that, if they cannot compete, at least will serve us and sever us from dependence whilst creating local jobs and prosperity. This will go hand in hand with understanding each other's view point to build relationships, thus avoiding preconceived ideas and assumptions; hence, by grouping stakeholders or partners and countries in the power/interest matrix, we could produce a better picture of how communication as well as relationships between us and the west have affected our prospect and progress up to this stage. A solution will be at hand and a clear picture on the way forward will be found when our education system has been reshaped to educate aware minds, thus producing people who understand where we are going and who we are. Nothing is preventing us from coming out with an educational system that has never been implemented elsewhere, which focuses on us and our future needs. After all, specialised education is more effective than a generic or general education or knowledge.

Our leadership and commitment

According to Abraham Lincoln, "Commitment is what transforms a promise into reality." It is my contention that citizens will always look up to their leaders to demonstrate that they are committed to change rather than just saying the words. Too often the leaders embrace change but their actions undermine it. So it appears for our continent today. Everyone chants change, every young person wants to see change happen but as soon as they get the opportunity to feed themselves, they abandon the cause.

Years ago, I spoke to a leader who inspired generations; at the end of his life, he accepted a ministerial post against his own ideology. I asked him why he did that. He told me that he has fought all his life and now he had been given the opportunity to be a minister, it is a dream for many that will never come true but for him, it was the moment.

He remained minister for over five years and never changed anything in his department, let alone in the country he alleged he was fighting for over a quarter of a century. Was this man an example we should all follow? I don't think so, but there is a lesson to learn from his action. From inside, it is possible to understand the cracks and fix them if we are not too concerned about our personal benefits. It is often difficult to fight a system from the outside; if this can be done, this is ideal, but our best enemies are those who are closer to us, because they know our weaknesses and strengths. Therefore, we should keep our worst enemies close. This is exactly what I was saying using the power and interest matrix. The second lesson is that a politician who cannot change his position is not worthy of any trust. Why? Because time changes and positions need to be adjusted to remain current; however, our vision should remain focused on the ideal, on what appears to be the best and most selfless calculated gain. The vision is what attracts people and it is what creates followership. Without a vision, people perish; or 'my people perish for lack of vision', says the Bible.

I am of the view that like every organisation, every country requires a clear long-term vision in order to secure stakeholders' commitment, and so it is for every country which requires short–medium term goals and objectives. I am not advocating for 50 year contracts, no! I am talking about the country planning for 50 years and beyond with its citizens on board. In business, for example, there are different levels of strategies; at the corporate level you have the overall vision which is then cascaded into each department and business units. This should be the same for a country, that the overall goals can easily be cascaded down to each citizen in the way that they are able to understand where the country is going and what they need to do as individuals to partake to that vision. If each citizen is clear about their role, they will help us run the country in the way we planned and we will reach our expected outcomes for everyone's benefit.

I am also proposing a conference on Africa where all African countries are gathered together to discuss their future destinies, not just through the AU. If it is within the AU because we don't want to reinvent the wheel, the organisation will have to be revamped and stop taking funding from western countries. African nations should be able to fund their organisation and projects. There is money in Africa. Each country should pay their membership as required. Many fail to do so. A totally different framework where support is not sought from any other sources than Africa is required. Another framework between Africa and the west, including the USA, hosted by Africa in Africa, should take place to discuss abuses of the past, reparation management and a way forward. The USA and Europe both have to pay for slavery as they all benefited from and committed it. The only difference is that some used the income to stay and others brought slavery income back home to their respective countries of origin, and this income helped each party. During this conference, a frank discussion should be put on the table and where there is something to address in Africa, it should be done with Africans and agreement reached with the west as to which sanctions a country should have if they infringe our rights and try to create internal troubles in our countries.

Many people don't know, and I think it is good for us to mention, that many African countries don't pay their fee to the AU and most AU projects and positions are financed by the west; this makes it difficult to take certain positions. Why should we continue to depend on others when we have everything? Why should we continue to beg and want our independence? We can have our AU at the size we want and in relation to our means and abilities. For positions that we cannot fund, we can use our volunteers or retired willing citizens to fill them and where necessary reduce the salaries to the size we can support.

We need a leadership commitment in this area and someone to push ahead for integration without delay. The idea about becoming united in the mid-term is too frightening, at least for now because people will tend to protect whichever advantage and power they have, but a proper integration can be done without delay starting with free movement of people and goods. We can trade amongst ourselves as I have already discussed. The sooner we start to trade amongst ourselves, we will realise that we have a huge market of one billion consumers, bigger than the Euro zone. Through trading and free movement of people and goods, we will be able to attract the brains that we need within the continent and new opportunities will open up. Yes, at the beginning, some countries may receive more migrants than others, but it has been proven that the influx of migrants will also create opportunities and more wealth for that nation. Conditions should be put in place to encourage this. This is where someone should take the lead, not as a president, but people can be paid and given a full green light to do this.

I know there are various structures in place in Africa; they are working the way they are but they can be revamped, changed or improved. The new structure should take into consideration our cultures and current blockers of progress, for example: it is easier for a proper integration to take place in West Africa than in Central Africa. It is easier to engage people in West Africa than in Central Africa. In Central Africa, people are more concerned about what they will get individually rather than what the whole sub-region or the country will get. When there are meetings, they are more concerned about per diem and salaries than success and this culture should be discouraged in a polite, positive and professional way because we are building and should avoid dissentions. It is also clear that in Central Africa, a director will not allow or agree to a project that does not benefit his personal interests. This is because these people are used to the culture of national self-help and corruption, so proper checks and balance should be put in place.

Our integration programme should be supported by vigilance as western countries will start proposing funding for one project or another or a particular aspect of our programme. As we already know that aid is always self-orientated and never without conditions. So we must stay away from aid because we are able to manage our own destinies. Not that it will not be difficult, but I am sure one billion people can do more than 500 million come together. If we are vigilant. Our vigilance will include our ability to have good intelligence services; however, knowing that we don't control the internet or telephone systems, it will be up to us to think what we should use to communicate amongst ourselves more effectively. There are brains within the continent to do this.

This is my proposal for changing the relationship spectrum, but it is also a political programme; not that I want to run for power, but this does not exclude any such attempts in the future, nonetheless, this is an ideal that I am sure at least for now we can aim for our continent. I have travelled in many countries, discussed with many young and old Africans and they are all Africanists. They like the continent; they want Africans to do more and to offer more than what it currently offers. They want it to stand out more than it currently does, they want the continent to think, behave and act more with a sense of responsibility and togetherness. Yes, this is because we all understand that, alone, the battle is lost. The battle to overcome our individual challenges and beyond. We are now ready to exercise our freedom, now that we have uncovered what bound us. We are ready, now having understood where our true battle lies. Our true battle was in our minds and we were ignorant servants working harder than donkeys for other people's interests, having been preconditioned and programmed unconsciously to serve. Our right to think freely was taken away from us, long before we started learning foreign languages. We didn't know that those who were laughing with us, showing so much compassion and sympathising with us were doing so as part of a plan to maintain us where we were. It is now clear, we are now awake and understand the trap, we are ridding ourselves of preprogrammed and concealed plans to reduce us to bless yes, yes. We are no longer serving, we are now taking full control. Above the Colonial Subconscious, Africa Moves. This is it. We stand tall now and hold up to the hope that we have always had and will look at what strengths we have with optimism. It is our time to take charge, like we did in the beginning. We are the ancestors of all, no one can deny this; let's command the respect we deserve.

Chapter 17:

Moving Beyond Colonial Confinement

The subconscious mind is the repository of acts that are either learned or internalised overtime, which in a long run dictates and guides our behaviour and actions. It has been discovered that our subconscious stores for later retrieval, information that the conscious mind may not immediately process with full understanding. I would say that our subconscious mind contains something like computer software for our involuntary functions, emotions, and habits.

The Colonial power knew quite well that the subconscious mind is a composite of everything one sees, hears and any information the mind collects that may not be consciously processed to make meaningful sense first hand. The conscious mind cannot always absorb disconnected information; therefore the subconscious mind stores this information where it can be retrieved when it needs it to defend itself for survival, for solving problems or for normal daily life.

With its ability to influence everything we do, our subconscious mind can and should be a great ally in achieving success in life, but equally, it can bring our downfall. It is clear henceforth that vices like laziness, poverty, fear or lack are products of our mind and their real source can be traced to the teaching our education or our upbringing.

When we have internalised the types of experiences that can impact negatively in our life, the appropriate cure should be the change of our mind-set. This requires another set of opposite education which enforces our ability to believe in ourselves in order to overcome fear, self-rejection or low self-esteem. It follows that negative experiences should therefore be overcome with positive thinking.

With this understanding, I conclude that most of African people's habits and emotional conditioning were programmed either in early childhood or throughout their education. Education is what we learn formally and informally. My contention is that, in order to secure their interests in their various colonies, western powers had vested interest in moulding African people's behavioural pattern. Through their programmes and conditioning, they modified the African's behaviour in a way that could not hinder their interests.

As already explained elsewhere in this book, the colonial power went to Africa to stay and to exercise control, they needed to ensure that things worked to their advantages. Every system they put in place was to help them perpetuate their goal and take as much advantage as possible. Conditioning African people's mind in a way that kept them dependent and captive was one of their priorities. They knew how human psychology works and they knew that people are driven by emotions. Systems that appealed to African people's emotions such as insults, putting them down, bullying them, ridiculing them, blaming them, pitying them, sympathising with them, getting them to betray their fellow citizens, appearing to be seen as helpers and pretending to care for them was part of the strategy to appeal to their emotion.

In reality they only cared for themselves. You cannot care for someone whilst occupying his land without permission; you cannot care for people you are exploiting; you cannot say you care for people you are killing. In reality, the prime reason behind schools, hospitals, religion and administrative system that were put in place was to raise a generation of helpers and followers; a generation of servants and dependents.

When African people were being trained and educated, colonial educators expected them to act and make decisions based on the training they received. Africans were expected to act as the masters expected, and they surely started to act as planned. The Plan was working!

For those who are still not clear, I take a simple example. Our parents give us certain upbringing to help us function in the way they wished. It follows that our behaviour is determined by what we were trained to believe. So when we are in front of certain situations, when we are faced with danger for example, our mind recalls what it has internalised as mechanism of defiance to respond appropriately.

I take another example: children that have been spoon fed to the adulthood will run to mum or dad when they are hungry, and those who are regularly cared for will seek attention every time they are in need of care.

When someone is provided with solutions every time they are in need, they tend to go back to the solution bringer every time there is an issue to resolve. When someone gets medication and cure for a disease from somewhere, he will go back there every time he is sick. As we can see, in all areas of their life, African people depend on the west for answers: medicine, invention, technology, political system, education, administrative systems, trade, international relations, date and timing, algebra, finances and banking, insurance, communication, practically every area, they turn to the west for solutions. Does this mean that African people cannot do anything by themselves? Absolutely not! They had their calendar, their medicine, their judicial system, and their government and communication systems before the invasion. But all this was abandoned. In fact, they were forced to abandon them because if they had kept them, the colonial powers wouldn't have been able to control them.

With their readymade solutions, planned and aimed at keeping African people dependent, they conditioned them to the point that even gone, African people have become unable to undertake anything by themselves. With this picture in mind, African people have now concluded that they cannot do anything because they will not be allowed. Africans cry and chant and ask for the transfer of technologies, a word used in the wrong context. Technology transfer refers to the process of transferring discoveries and innovations resulting from university research to the commercial sector. But I hear African people requesting the transfer in almost all their debates. They are always asking for the west to transfer technologies. The transfer from the west to the south is not possible. Can't we develop research centres in our own universities and get them to make discoveries that can be transferred to our commercial sector?

People, who know how the capitalist system works, understand quite well that the transfer will not happen. Non one will transfer their inventions to Africa for free. They conceive and invent things for a purpose and the main drive is to meet the needs whilst making money in the process. Sometimes, they have spent billion in the project and they will not give it for free unless they have made their money back. Someone has to pay for it unless it is useless. African people have to understand that nothing they receive is free unless it is useless!

So why do all Africans people, no matter where I go, from Kenya to Uganda, from Chad to Benin, from Togo to Ghana, from Ivory Coast to Burkina Faso, From Mali to Senegal, from Nigeria to Cameroon expect solutions from the former colonial powers? The answer is simple! They have been trained and conditioned to act in this way and as long as they continue to act in this way, they will remain enslaved, under developed and poor.

African people think they are free and conscious of their actions when in reality they are not. Lets' explain this using the contest of training. At the beginning of any training, our actions are conscious but the more we repeat the training, the more we internalise the process unconsciously to the point that we master the ability to perform the most difficult tasks without much efforts. In fact the longer we learn and apply what we have learned, the more our mind and body become accustomed to it, our mind and actions become coordinated. Musicians who practice regularly will play well even with their eyes closed.

Also what happens to people who are abused? They resist at the beginning but the more they are subjected to the same fate, the more they become used to abuses and it comes a point where abuses become acceptable and normal thing for them. This is why it is easy for people who have been abused to become abusers themselves.

So why is Africa poor despite the so called efforts? It is because they are still mentally and psychologically bound, having been trained to accept, see and consider themselves as poor people. Their nature rejects poverty but their subconscious mind accepts it. Unconsciously they have decided to remain poor and they are constantly distracted to find the causes of poverty elsewhere instead of looking inwardly to discover their source of wealth.

Without a good diagnosis, an illness will never be cured. Similarly, without understanding the causes of poverty, Africa will never become rich and free. African people have been trained to look outward for the causes of poverty, whilst success and freedom is spiritual, psychological and requires psychological strategies for their attainment.

How did we become so foolish? Whilst our human reason does bears witness with our conscious mind that we are free, the spirit of laziness, coupled with lies and ideologies urge us to look elsewhere for solutions for our problems.

If we think carefully we will realise that those who came out with programmes to dominate Africa positioned themselves as the ultimate solution bringers. People look out to them as those who can help. By looking out to them for solutions, they become dependent. Being dependent of the colonial power for most of our needs means that we consider them as masters, thus giving them the power to control us at will.

The former colonial masters therefore think faster as they continue to develop better and sophisticated methods to keep African people dependent. Our dependence on them makes them great, prosperous. They make their living on Africa's demise, their prosperity depends on people's ability to follow them but they will never tell us the truth. They make African people's believe that they will die if they fail to do as expected. This is not true! We can do all things; however, overcoming psychological enslavement requires a psychological breakthrough.

African people's efforts should therefore focus on things that they need that they don't control. That is what the west does. This is what China is doing. All treaties, partnerships, agreements are all geared towards controlling things that they need which are not under their control. If Africa needs clothing, sugar, TV sets, or anything that they genuinely think that they need, they need a strategy to control them in some way.

In this book I have proposed many ways we can redefine our way and redesign our systems. New structures will imposed a certain psychological behaviour, and the more we start to behave in a new way, the easier our subconscious will internalised our new behaviour; and the more this behaviour infiltrates our subconscious, the easier we will become confident in ourselves, our abilities and our possibilities.

From within we will change our life and social conditions and as we reject pity, aid, and sympathy, we will become proud people, finding solutions to our problems.

Moving above the colonial subconscious is a giant step that African people are taking. By cleansing their minds, they will impose new ways going forward. Africans can build bridges and mega infrastructures, invent heavy machineries, discover new technologies, cars, air planes, and find new medicines. Africans can breakthrough in every area. Africans can do much more than what they can actually see or think as long as they agree that all things are possible. Africans are moving beyond the colonial confinement and self-imposed limitations.

To move beyond self-imposed limitations, requires some principles starting with the imagination of an ideal situation sustained by a new vision. This new vision will need to be guided by key milestones and a self-evaluation and monitoring processes for each stage need to be set up from a short, mid to long terms.

Our plan can go from a year to over fifty years. The

most important thing for us was to understand what binds Africa and we are now fully aware of what has kept this continent down for over 60 years after our independence's. We know people's mind was conditioned and tricked. Now we are getting rid of all these lies. From now on, each African should doubt about everything the west proposes like Descartes suggested; assessing thoroughly every gestures and every acts of the former colonial powers. Every offer will be assessed, and I am proposing to doubt about the genuineness and sincerity of their motives. We need to doubt about all their moves, their offers, their gestures, their gifts and surprises. Equally, we will think carefully before we act.

We need to remember that only individual actions will create a collective state of our society. Therefore, each of us should be the African we want to see in others. We need to be that person we want to see in a student, public sector worker, professor, teacher, farmer, minister, police office, taxi driver, or a doctor. Whether we are a doctors, police officer, farmer, public sector worker, professor, teacher, researcher, student or driver, we should be the ideal person we want to see in these professions.

If we are all the ideal person we wish for our position, we will create the ideal society we want to build. Even within our profession, we should keep in mind that we may not necessarily be fulfilling our purpose. Therefore, beside our normal jobs, we may have a burning desire to do something else. If this is the case, we should continue to work at it and dig within ourselves to identify our purpose in life. If each of us achieves his purpose, we will build a better society. We need to make our dream and passion come true. We need to think it, live it, work at it and believe in it, casting away every spirit of fear and doubts about our abilities by constantly reaffirming to ourselves that we can do all things.

If we try and fail, we should try again and again and again until we have succeeded. After all, successful people have a catalogue of failures. Only their last move propelled them to the house of fame. We need to remember that the world celebrates people's success without knowing the story behind. A Better Africa's dream is not dead, and as long as we still believe in a better future and work at it, we will surely get there. We remember President Abraham Lincoln for his achievements but some of us know how his successes are fewer compared to his failures. Funnily, he is still remembered today because his fewer successes over shadowed his failures. Let's look at his curriculum Vitae!

In 1831, Abraham Lincoln lost his job

In 1832, Abraham Lincoln wanted to be a senator, but he was defeated

In 1833, his business went bankrupt, so he failed in business

In 1834, Abraham Lincoln had a manior breakthrough when he was elected to Illinois State as legislature.

In 1835, Abraham Lincoln lost the woman he loved, he nearly went mad

In 1836, he has a nervous breakdown affected by the death of his lover

In 1838, he stood election for Illinois House Speake, but he lost

In 1843, he was again defeated in run for nomination for U.S.A Congress

In 1846, he was finaly elected to Congress

In 1848, he lost for the nomination as presidential candidate for his party

In 1849, he was rejected for land officer position

In 1854 he was defeated in run for U.S.A Senate

In 856 he was defeated in run for nomination for Vice President

In 1858, Abraham Lincoln was again defeated in run for U.S.A Senate

In 1860, Abraham Lincoln was finally elected President of the USA. He became president in the United State of America. What a journey! Despite his defeats, we never gave up and kept believing and kept trying.

This last success put him in a position where he impacted not only his country but the world. It is also said that without his failures, Thomas Edison might not have become America's most well-known and prolific innovator.

Remember my time in the wilderness, trolling through the bushes from Mengan to Sa'a Nzock, 18 kilometres every day from home to school and back; remember me, Ben Mengan, not giving up despite my childhood poverty, not giving up despite the struggle to get my passport; remember our very first day back to the village when my Dad, Mbii Mengan was discharged from army and how we returned home with nothing, remember that what kept me going was the hope that I had for a better future and my desire to break mental barriers. I refused to accept that certain things were beyond my reach. For the same reasons, I believe in a better Africa, a free Africa and a prosperous Africa.

This is why we need to be a good news bringer, wherever we find ourselves, we need to talk positively about Africa, avoid resentment about the west, praise good things they have done and aspire to do more than what they have done. We need to treat every human being with respect. We need to respect other people's inventions because we have all benefited from their work. What they have done has advanced the world and our civilisation: lets' not dwell in the past. What was keeping us down is now known and we still have what it takes to be who we want.

Africa is on the move to the top, beyond the colonial subconscious, Africans are moving. Moving beyond imposed limitations and armed with self-belief. By setting up personal challenges, each of us will become the change we want to see in others.

We are all change agents and our actions will impact others. Our way of life will serve as witness and testimony. Let us not just claim that one African has achieved in the space development, this single example is not enough. We are better than this and these isolated examples are too few as percentage amongst 1 billions genius people. Put on a chart, they will not be readable! In the chart of achievement, we should be comparing ourselves to the Japanese, Chinese, American, Europeans as we are all equally able to achieve whatever any human being can achieve.

The world is still in construction and better discoveries are still to come. This is why we need to look around us and think critically to identify problems that we can solve. We should find ways to meet our needs by ourselves. To mimic Pastor Matthew Ashimlowo, we need to see the gaps around us and ask ourselves what needs are there, and how we can meet them. We need to ask ourselves, what will be required in the process meeting those needs and how long it may take to get there. We may not get there straight away and we may face setbacks and failures. If we do, we can only be sure of one thing: one more push can be the last push to glory.

We are not late; we are simply on our way to the top. The 21st century is just the start of our glory and the 22nd century will be fully African's. Africa is preparing to take charge, teach the world, invent new technologies, provide resources, feed the world and set moral standard whilst bringing the world back to God and to fundamental values that human being needs as rulers of the earth.

Our belief is now unwavering and without doubt. We will get there; we are the chosen generations, peculiar people, moving above all forms of subjugations. Our individual endeavours will create a state of collective achievement that can no longer be ignored. Our cries are over. We just needed a small lift, a simple reminder that we could do everything. This reminder has achieved it goad and has lifted our spirit. This reminder has broken the barriers that were holding us down. We advance and move far beyond the cliché of the colonial era.

Some of us just can't believe that the solution was so simple! We say that every solution has always been simple, the difficulties are in the process of reaching the solution; however, the truth was always ready and waiting to be discovered. Now that we have discovered the truth, we are free and let's live it, and own it. We have freed our last area of bondage, our mind! We are now free from inside out. We now take our banner and lift it higher- our memorandum of hope - which is now our guiding principle to the top.

I therefore offer you this Memorandum of Hope, our guiding principle for action.

Why a Memorandum of Hope? I chose to call this last part of the book a Memorandum of Hope because of the nature of the message I want to convey. A memorandum is a short note designating something to be remembered, especially something to be done or acted upon in the future. The memorandum is also a record or written statement of something or an informal message, especially between two or more people belonging to the same organisation, country or continent, concerning the continent or country's business or direction. This memorandum is for Africa and it is our Memorandum of Hope, from me to you.

To all of you who love Africa, your unconditional love will not go to waste as long as you continue to believe that change is possible. Here it is, your memorandum of hope.

Chapter 18:

Memorandum of Hope

A Memorandum of Hope from me, to you

Today is a new day which brings a new vision and hope to us all Africans.

Our midnight is now but forever brighter than noon and we see afar with an unobstructed vision.

The past we dwell in it no longer, and we visit it just to learn and revise our actions of today.

However, we forget not to claim what is due to us. We will get a full refund of what we lost and we vow not to repeat our errors of yesterday.

Our children, forced to work for free are expecting their share of the wealth they created. We wait for you to name the price for the damage!

We end the cries because we see the price of our sacrifices- the west and north was built by us.

The wealth they hold is partly ours. We claim our share!

Yesterday, we lacked the courage to name and shame, but today is a new day.

Today is a day of hope! Hope to lead the way like we did in the past.

Today is a new day; we are fully awake and aware of

what is going on.

We have learnt from our past mistakes and we know where we got it wrong.

We are not afraid to start afresh, the steps to take no matter how long they are, will soon be overcome.

We will rise and walk again despite the fall, and where possible we will run to recoup the time lost.

The path to there, we know less, yet the point to reach we know it well.

As long as we will, the hurdles are less our worries, but along the way we will renew our minds, seeking to discover the truth in all what we do.

We will no longer act in haste and sell in a rush, we will sleep and think about our future before we act and, as far as possible, we will find the best way to use what Mother Nature endowed us as resources.

We live for now but see afar, through our foresight, and know the best is ahead, so, we act to secure the best for our future. Today is already gone. Tomorrow matters much as we plan ahead with care; we leave nothing to chance.

Our kids will get the best, if we take the steps required today, but for them to remain awake, they need to know the truth.

This is brought to light wherever to go to learn, how they tricked our minds, so for them to remain awake to avoid he same mistakes.

Our faults and wrongs have taught us and shape our drive and our resolve is to be ourselves as we rid ourselves of lies and packs loads we carried for years unaware.

We lack nothing we need, but if it was the case, despite the lacking of now, our mind is for there, the vision we have in mind, we see the state we want reach.

As long as heirs remain in the land, for sure we'll climb the mount to the top, our rightful place from where we we ought to command respect.

For sure we'll see our will and hope come to pass.

The mess of now is naught but clues for what we need to leave behind.

It's not the time to walk like crabs, but to set our minds and eyes and drive to the same direction our feet are taking, now and forevermore.

The fire behind chases us ahead and sackcloths are laid down along the way

As we wear now ones to press ahead.

Because we know the cool we'll meet ahead, the heat of now is less our worry.

It's time to dream and act with urge, and reach to take with hands of faith, what for so long we dreamed to get.

What our spirit sees, we have a mouth to call it to be.

For what we call for sure will come to pass as long as we believe without a doubt.

So long as we break the veil of impossibility, which is nothing but the limit we impose on ourselves..

Now that we are sure nothing can stop us, the time is set and the clock can start.

Here and now our move to win, for sure our plans will come to being.

For those of doubt, we leave behind because our purpose is to clear the way

and release the best from those with us.

For our belief is all we need for now.

As long as we have a plan to cross the bridge,

The way to there will clear itself.

The hope ahead will be our guide

The point to reach we know for sure;

But all we need we know not now, but as long as we move and press forth,

Ideas will follow and shape the plan we need for next

and when we are there, we'll know for sure.

If we miss the point, the world we tell because by then they'll know our plans.

We were the first on earth, first to strive for the best, first to teach the world and first to give and first to lead the way. Our time of slumber has elapsed and we retake our place.

We come from where everyone wants to be and have all that everyone wants to have. We are truly in a paradise, let's recognise and enjoy it as we move above all sorts of subjugations, prejudices and plans to belittle us.

We now know who we are, the best, the chosen and the privileged.

No one will and can tell us otherwise. This is why from all corners of the earth all pretend to be our friends, so as to get a bit of what we have. We will now only give on our terms.

We are created in the image of God, perfect in potential.

It's up to us to release that potential, to perfect our course; we have the ability to do it.

We are moving above as heads, not tails. That's what Africa is!

References and Bibliography

Acemoglu, Daron, Johnson, Simon & Robinson, James A. (2002) Reversal of Fortune: Geography and Institutions in the Making of the Modern World Income Distribution; *Quarterly Journal of Economics*, 117(November):1231–1294.

Argandoña, A. (1998). The Stakeholder Theory and the Common Good; *Journal of Business Ethics*,17:1093-1102.

Bourne, L. & Walker, D.H.T. (2005). Visualising and Mapping Stakeholder Influence; *Management Decision*, 43(5):649-660.

Briner, W., Geddes, M. & Hastings, C. (1996). *Project Leadership*; 2nd ed., Gower Publishing Co.

Bunn, M.D., Savage, G.T. & Holloway, B.B. (2002). Stakeholder Analysis for Multi-Sector Innovations; *The Journal of Business and Industrial Marketing*, 17(2/3):181–203.

Chan, A.P.C., Chan, D.W.M., Fan, L.C.N., Lam, P.T.I. & Yeung, J.F.Y. (2006). Partnering for Construction Excellence – A Reality or Myth? *Building and Environment*, 41:1924-1933.

Clarke, T. (1998). The Stakeholder Corporation: A Business Philosophy for the Information Age; *Long Range Planning*, 31(2):182-194.

Clarkson, M.B. (1995). A Stakeholder Framework for Analysing and Evaluating Corporate Social Performance; *Academy of Management Review*, 20:39-48.

Clement, R.W. (2005). The Lessons from Stakeholder Theory for U.S. Business Leaders; *Business Horizons*, 48:255-264.

Colacoglu S, Lepak D.P &Hong(2006) Public Management Review, 12(5), 609–634. Coff, RW (1997). Human assets and management dilemmas: Coping with hazards on the road to resource-based theory. Academy of Management Review, 22(2), 374–402. Elliott, R.K. (1967). Socrates and Plato D.P & . *Kant-Studien* 58(18n): 138.

Fall, Babacar (1993). *Le travail forcé en Afrique occidentale française*, 1900-1945. Paris: Karthala.

Gatens, Moira and Lloyd, Genevieve (1999) *Collective Imaginings: Spinoza, Past and Present*. Routledge. ISBN 978-0-415-16570-9, ISBN 978-0-415-16571-6.

Goldstein, Rebecca (2006). *Betraying Spinoza: The Renegade Jew Who Gave Us Modernity*. Schocken. ISBN 978-0-8052-1159-7.

Goode, Francis (2012). *Life of Spinoza*. Smashwords edition. ISBN 978-1-4661-3399-0.

Gullan-Whur, Margaret (1998). *Within Reason: A Life of Spinoza.* Jonathan Cape. ISBN 978-0-224-05046-3.

Hall, Dale (1980). Interpreting Plato's Cave as an Allegory of the Human Condition; Apeiron: *A Journal for Ancient Philosophy and Science,* 14(2):74–75. Retrieved 10 December 2014.

Hampshire, Stuart (1951). *Spinoza and Spinozism.* OUP, 2005. ISBN 978-0-19-927954-8.

Hardt, Michael (trans.) (2011) University of Minnesota Press. Preface, in French, by Gilles Deleuze. Available here: Multitudes Web - 01. Préface à L'Anomalie sauvage de Negri. Multitudes.samizdat.net. Archived from the original on 11 June 2011. Retrieved 2 May 2011.

Israel, Jonathan (2001). *The Radical Enlightenment.* Oxford: Oxford University Press, 2006.

Israel, Jonathan. (2006), *Enlightenment Contested: Philosophy, Modernity, and the Emancipation of Man* 1670–1752. ISBN 978-0-19-927922-7.

Ives, David (2009) *New Jerusalem: The Interrogation of Baruch de Spinoza at Talmud Torah Congregation: Amsterdam,* July 27, 1656. New York: Dramatists Play Service, Inc. ISBN 978-0-8222-2385-6.

John B. Watson (1878–1958) – *Popularizing Behaviorism, The Little Albert Study, The "Dozen Healthy Infants", Life after the University.* Available here: http://education.stateuniversity. com/pages/2543/Watson-John-B-1878-1958.html

Lewin, K. (1939). When Facing Danger. In Lewin, G.W. (Ed.), *Resolving Social Conflict*. London: Harper & Row.

Lewin, K. (1943a). Psychological Ecology. In Cartwright, D. (Ed.), *Field Theory in Social Science*. London: Social Science Paperbacks.

Lewin, K. (1943b). The Special Case of Germany. In Lewin, G.W. (Ed.), *Resolving Social Conflict*. London: Harper & Row.

Lewin, K. (1943–44). Problems of Research in Social Psychology. In Cartwright, D. (Ed.), *Field Theory in Social Science*. London: Social Science Paperbacks.

Lewin, K. (1946). Action Research and Minority Problems. In Lewin, G.W. (Ed.), *Resolving Social Conflict*. London: Harper & Row.

Lewin, K. (1947a). Frontiers in Group Dynamics. In Cartwright, D. (Ed.), *Field Theory in Social Science*. London: Social Science Paperbacks.

Lewin, K. (1947b). Group Decisions and Social Change. In Newcomb, T.M. and Hartley, E.L. (Eds), *Readings in Social Psychology*. New York: Henry Holt.

Maslow, A. (1954). *Motivation and personality*. New York, NY: Harper. pp. 91

Medlow, A. L. (1978) "Strategic Planning for Harper and Row, New York, New Organizational Effectiveness-- The York," Long Range Ross, G. H. B. and Goodfellow, J. L. "A Planning.

Mendelow, A. (1991) 'Stakeholder Mapping', Proceedings of the 2nd International Conference on Information Systems, Cambridge, MA (Cited in Scholes, 1998

Palmer, Robin H. & Parsons, Neil (Eds) (1977). *The Roots of Rural Poverty in Central and Southern Africa*. Berkeley and Los Angeles: University of California Press.

Watt, Stephen (1997). *Introduction: The Theory of Forms (Books 5–7), Plato*: *Republic*. London: Wordsworth Editions, pp. xiv–xvi. ISBN 1-85326-483-0.

Author Biography

Michel Ngue-Awane is an innovative, dynamic and forward-thinking individual with a background in Philosophy, Psychology, Theology and business. He is a Commissioning and Procurement Consultant and a member of the Chartered Institute of Purchasing and Supply (CIPS).

Michel holds a Bachelor and Masters in Philosophy and Politics and he obtained his MBA from London Metropolitan University before starting a professional Doctorate in Social Work at Tavistock & Portman NHS which he deferred to focus on his business. He also holds a Diploma in Christian ministries from KCE.

Ngue-Awane has won many awards including the Millennium Award with a lifetime fellowship and UNLTD Award. His first book Practice Guide to Social Housing (2009) was acclaimed by housing professionals in the United Kingdom. He runs a number of different businesses including his own brand PEP Chilli Sauce which is sold across the UK and has written over 100 songs.